1

One Horsewoman to Another

By

Sheri Grunska

Trading in Your High Heels

For Muddy Work Boots and Finding

Courage, Confidence and Joy in All Of It!

Edited by Martha Schultz

Front Cover photo by Leah Gloudemans
Photography assistant – Nicole Kohanski

"She is clothed with strength and dignity and she laughs without fear of the future"
Proverbs 31:25

To my daughters Kaeli and Lauren

What an amazing journey you both have just begun in life. No matter what you choose to do for a career, always be true to your heart and embrace the very special gifts both of you were given long before you were born. You will use those gifts for many wonderful purposes throughout your entire life. What beautiful women you are becoming.

Acknowledgments

This book has been a complete joy to write and even though thoughts come flying out of my head and unto paper, most of it would not be understandable without the help of others that have a gift in editing. I want to thank Martha Schultz for reading my book several times and editing it. Your honest feedback has helped me to look deeper inside myself to find the right words to express what I want to say. Thank you for all your work on this book.

I am blessed to have friends that are willing to read my work even when they are extremely busy with their own career and family. From the bottom of my heart I want to thank Cindy Lambert for taking the time to read this book. Your encouragement and willingness to listen to me when I start to feel insecure about what I am trying to say has been an incredible gift to me. Thank you!

I want to thank my husband David for always supporting me no matter what idea I have going on in my head. You are always willing to pick up the slack when I am writing and that means a lot more work for you here at the farm. You are my rock and I love you.

Table of Contents

The Reason I Wrote This Book

From high heels to very muddy work boots! No one could have ever prepared me for the journey I was about to go on as a woman when we opened our boarding stable. My husband David and I built Vinland Stables back in 2005 and it was one of the most exciting times in my life. I was living the dream. Taking care of other people's horses seemed like the perfect career choice and I was ready for it all. I had left the world I knew behind and that included nice (clean) clothes, make-up and hair done daily and friends at my workplace. But I was ready (or least I thought I was) to start a new career full-time on our horse farm. I had endless energy and along with my husband we wanted to make our boarding barn the perfect place for everyone. I envisioned my two young daughters growing up around horses and becoming part of the business and loving it as much as I did. I also envisioned my new career being somewhat easy because I had worked at a couple of horse barns in my life and I thought I had a good idea of what I was doing. After all, how much different could it possibly be as the barn owner instead of the employee?

My life changed overnight as the horses started filling our stalls and outdoor board. When it was done I was caring for forty horses at our barn and I was shocked to say the least. Things changed dramatically in just a few short days and at that moment I was not able to fully grasp what we had gotten ourselves into. I was so busy and my days were packed with doing chores, making sure our new boarders were situated and happy and of course taking care of my very young daughters. This would be my world for the next few years before I started to realize that there was more to life than the horses and I needed to have a life outside the barn from time to time.

After all these years I still love what I do and I don't regret starting our business but that is not how I felt during the first couple of years running our boarding barn. I dropped off the face of the earth to all those that knew me outside the barn and horse world because I was just too busy and somewhere in all of it I lost myself and who I was.

Looking back, the first five years of running our barn are now just a blur. I don't remember where the time went and I missed out on so much because the business took precedence over everything including my marriage and even my girls from time to time.

Things needed to change and they needed to change from within me. I had to find myself again and once I did I became a much better barn owner and barn manager, wife, mother and friend. My family became number one again and I learned to run my barn without guilt or pressure. I learned to make decisions for the betterment of the barn and business and it was okay if not everyone agreed. I learned that my barn will not be for everyone and that is fine. Clients will leave and others will come and I realized that through all of it I have survived and come out stronger as a businesswoman.

The reason I wrote this book is because I now know that everything I went through during the early years is common for many women who decide to start a business. The truth is that it is unbelievably hard. I now have the privilege of talking with many wonderful women from all over the country. They have the same dream I had many years ago. They love horses and have a deep desire to run their own horse business. What they have come to find out way too soon is the emotional side of dealing with the business is extremely difficult. The stress of conflict and learning to run a business starts to steal the joy that they had in the beginning. Hurt feelings become all too real and, for women, we just can't turn it off very easily. The job will emotionally consume us and burn us out if we are not careful. I hear in the voices of many of these women the same panic and stress that I had experienced. They are overwhelmed in their business, everything has become much more difficult than they ever imagined and they don't see a way out. Becoming a professional horsewoman was not supposed to be like this!

This book is perfect for women of any age that want to start a horse business or are already deep into it. It doesn't matter if you are running a large facility or boarding a couple of horses at your home. The struggles and challenges are very real and will be similar for both. This book is about finding yourself again and becoming the confident businesswoman you know you are inside. I am so glad I didn't give up on my dream. I love my career more than ever now and I still love going out to the barn. The horses are still the best part of the job and it makes me happy seeing my clients out in the barn each day.

You are about to embark on an incredible journey as a professional horsewoman and through it all you will learn so much about yourself both good and maybe not so good. Embrace it all and get ready for the ride of your life.

~A special note~

As I was writing this book I started to feel a flood of emotions surface from the past all the way until present. I have changed in many ways and my goals have changed also. I now understand that this is something that we all will experience as we become businesswomen.

I felt that it was very important to add extra pages at the end of each chapter with thought provoking questions to get you digging deep inside your heart and soul. You might say you can keep it as a personal journal of your plans, struggles and triumphs along the way. Years from now you will enjoy looking at it and seeing how far you have come.

This book is perfect to read alone or in a women's book club or study. It will lead to meaningful conversations with depth and the results will lead to growth as you learn more about yourself and what you want in your personal and business life. You might be very knowledgeable about horses but now it's time to learn about yourself and what you long to strive for in your professional and personal life.

Wishing you many blessings,
Sheri Grunska

~1~

Valley Girl

"We all start out as beginners in our journey to make our dreams come true"

I grew up in Los Angeles California during a much simpler time back in the sixties and seventies. My family bounced around from apartment to apartment and my only exposure to horses at such a young age came through the television. I fell in love with horses by watching old black and white westerns and then when Bonanza aired I was in heaven. Not only did I have a crush on Little Joe like so many other young girls but I loved his Pinto horse. I guess it would be true I was a valley girl all the way when the 1980's came.

In the 1970's there were lots of horses in the San Fernando Valley sprinkled between houses and apartment buildings. You could find horses pretty much anywhere back then and even though the valley was growing fast and buildings were going up at a rapid pace you could still see people riding horses in open fields that hadn't yet been covered by cement.

As a young girl I would have done anything to own a horse and it was something that I pestered my father about continuously. Finally when I was about ten years old I wore him down and he said we could look for a horse of my own.

My family knew absolutely nothing about horses and renting horses at Griffith Park was the extent of my hands-on experience. I thought I knew how to care for a horse because, after all, I had watched Bonanza and every horse movie that had aired back then. I came from the most non-horsey family you could ever imagine but I was a dreamer and my dreams never stopped even as I grew older.

After my father purchased my first horse I pretty much lived at the small boarding stable down the road during all my free time. I could ride my bike there after school and still get back in time for dinner and to do homework. I spent hours on the weekends with my horse Rusty and just like most young girls that own their first horse I was over the moon in love with him. During my waking hours I would constantly dream about having a career with horses.

Dreaming of a career

My first inspiration for having a career in horses came after I saw the movie National Velvet and I decided I wanted to jump horses in competition. That dream quickly faded because Rusty was a far cry from a jumper and he was more content just being lazy and eating everything in his sight. My next dream was to be a barrel racer and compete on the rodeo circuit. We gave that a try at some local horse shows but my horse was the slowest horse there and I had no idea what I was doing! We went to a few horse shows and did 4H and even though we never did very well, it didn't matter to me. I loved my horse and I thought he was perfect.

As I reached high school my riding improved and I had outgrown Rusty so we purchased a new very young horse. She was not broke when we got her and I fell in love all over again. I was about to learn a whole new level of horsemanship because she was not as easy going as Rusty. After a couple of years of owning and riding a very green young horse I thought (as many teenagers do) that I could become a trainer. After all how hard could it be? I had trained my first young unbroken horse and we made it through pretty easily and I just assumed that most horses were like this. I definitely had a lot to learn! I quickly found out that not all horses are the same and I was smart enough to realize that I was not cut out to be a horse trainer. I moved on to adult hood but the dreaming never stopped.

A different path

Life took a different path for me than what I wanted and I had to put my horse dreams on hold and get a real job. I had moved out of my father's house and of course had bills to pay. I was growing up and it seemed like my dreams and aspirations of working with horses for a living got further and further away. I tucked them away but never completely let go of them.

My dreams have changed many times over the years. I never expected to be boarding horses while in my forties and fifties let alone writing books about horse barn management and becoming an equine professional. Yet here I am many years later, far away from Los Angeles, California and the life I knew as a young girl. I now live on a horse farm in Wisconsin and my world is again all about horses. Now I am actually making a living doing what I love and I have the privilege of watching others work to achieve their goals and dreams with their horses.

It is not the career that I dreamed about as a girl. My days consist of doing morning chores and cleaning many stalls but I wouldn't trade it for the world. I am often in jeans that haven't been washed for a few days and sometimes I can't believe how dirty I can get especially during the muddy season. It is not glamourous at all but I know I am home and have a peace that I am where I am supposed to be. I can truly say I love what I do and have found complete contentment.

Dreams change and if you are open to seeing what is out there, you might be pleasantly surprised to find where life takes you. What is your dream? What if your dream changes in an unexpected way? Get ready because if you love horses and want to work with them, there are endless possibilities and opportunities. You just need to be open to the unexpected. Sometimes what God has planned for you will look different than what you have planned for your life and you just might find out that his plan is so much better.

Your Personal Goals

Before you get too far into this book, I encourage you to think about some of your goals and write them down here. Don't be surprised if they change as you get to the end of this book! Enjoy the journey!

Your Personal Thoughts

~2~

The Emotional Side
of Any Business

"Running a horse business is not for the faint of heart.
It's for the brave, the patient and the persistent.
It's for the professional horsewoman
waiting to be unleashed inside of you."

If you are planning on starting a horse business of any kind then let me tell you that starting it will be the easiest part. Planning how you want your barn to look and designing the tack room, stalls and arenas will consume you day and night. At least it did for me before we actually built our barn. I LOVED every minute of those times and I was on an emotional high pretty much every day.

I truly believe that women handle the events in their lives differently than men and building our barn and opening our boarding facility was no different. My husband David is the quiet type and he did what needed to be done each and every day just to get the barn and paddocks ready for horses. He may have been excited on the inside but he wasn't all crazy giddy on the outside like me.

I wore my emotions on the outside and if everything was going smoothly then I was on top of the world. If things were going badly (which they did pretty much throughout the entire construction process) then I was an emotional roller coaster and not only did my husband have to work every day trying to get things done, he had to contend with me. *Poor guy!*

I never really looked at myself as an up and coming businesswoman in those early days of starting our business. I felt more like a young naïve school girl getting ready to go on a ride at an amusement park with my best friend. Even when the stress was huge during the building of our barn and we found ourselves in two lawsuits with the builders, I still had not looked at myself as a businesswoman. I felt more like a victim and I held on to that for many years.

It would be a long time before I embraced the mistakes we made during the building process and took ownership of all of it as a businesswoman. Before that day would come there would be many tears, frustration and anger not just for what happened during the building construction but also because of all the stress that came with trying to run my barn during the first few years. I was trying to run a boarding barn but I really didn't know what I was doing when it came to dealing with clients. There were many issues and strong opinions about the barn and how I took care of the horses and I was not prepared any of it. The horses truly were the easiest part of the job.

The emotional roller coaster

I experienced every emotion that is conceivable in the beginning of our business venture and I was letting my emotions run my business and barn. I started off with complete happiness and confidence in what I was doing for the horses in my care and very quickly it turned into insecurity and frustration. I went through a period where I was angry all the time because I was put into situations that I was not mentally ready to handle when it came to my clients and their horses. There may have been good times sprinkled here and there during those early years but the difficult times definitely outweighed the easy days. It was an emotional roller coaster to say the least. Things wouldn't change until I changed and became the businesswoman and equine professional I needed to be to run a healthy and well-run boarding stable.

This is a journey that all women will go on when they work in any type of business. If you are going to own or manage a horse business then you are going to learn a lot about your strengths and weaknesses and you will need to dig deep to find the strength to keep going when things get tough. As women we want to do it all and many times we dive right in without a care in the world. In some ways this is what makes women unique and amazingly beautiful. God has given us a heart that is huge and can handle so much at one time.

As women we want to do it all and many times we dive right in without a care in the world. In some ways this is what makes women unique and amazingly beautiful. God has given us a heart that is huge and can handle so much at one time.

The journey you go on in your career with horses and clients will take you on many highs and lows but with each experience you will learn so much about yourself and what you can accomplish. You will also learn how to keep your emotions in check when you need to and what seemed so traumatic at one time, years later will feel like a moment in your life that was a simple bump in the road.

You will experience every emotion as you embark on your horse career but if you hang in there long enough and grow with each mistake, you will come full circle and you will become a different woman at the other end. It will be your choice on how you will arrive on the other end and your emotions will play a huge part in all of it.

Cold on the outside

Before we started boarding horses for a living I never gave much thought to the self-employed businesswoman and the life she has chosen in the business world. If I had any opinions about most professional women it was that they probably seemed a little cold on the outside. The journey they had been on throughout their career wasn't important to me at all and I was only interested in how they treated me when I worked for them.

All these years later I finally understand and can empathize with those women. They have taken a path that few travel and now I know it was not easy for most of them at one time or another. The emotional journey they have been on to get their business off the ground has molded them into who they are today and I am sure it left a few emotional scars along the way.

I wanted to share my story because once you hear it you will realize you are not alone. If you are just starting out then I hope this book will prepare you for what you may experience and know that it's going to be okay. How you run your barn and horse business in the beginning will change as time moves forward and you will change right along with it. Your learning curve will astound you, but most importantly you are going to learn so much about yourself. Every emotion you experience both good and bad will mold you into a confident equine professional and businesswoman if you allow it. Is it easy? I am going to be very honest and tell you that it is going to be extremely tough some days but you are stronger than anything that will be thrown at you. You just may not realize it yet.

Over the last thirteen years of running our boarding barn I can truly say I have experienced every emotion there is. In the beginning of our business venture I was euphoric and on cloud nine most of the time. When we opened our boarding barn things were wonderful for about a month or two. Yes, only a month or two! Business ownership reality had set in quickly and real issues started to evolve all around me and I was shaken to the core by the things I was now dealing with. I kept telling myself in the very beginning that it was just a onetime issue and tomorrow will be great. As each day came it brought new problems and new feelings that I had not experienced as a barn owner and manager. I kept trying to stay optimistic because, after all, how bad could it get? I had no idea at the time that I was going to be tested during the first three years of business ownership like never before. It is a completely different pressure when you are the owner of the business and no one can take the fall for you. You just can't pass all the problems on to someone else. You are it!

When I couldn't take the stress of all the issues we were having at the barn anymore I let my guard down and that allowed for many destructive emotions to grow inside of me. I feared they would bring me down to where I would never get up again. The emotions were strong and hard to deal with and I entered a new and unknown territory.

Insecurity and so much more

The emotions you will go through before, during and long into your business will be vast and change often especially at first. We are women and we already are very emotional to begin with. You will find yourself being happier than you have ever imagined and then angry and stressed without a moment's notice. You will want to cry (and probably will many times) and then pick yourself up and keep going. You will panic when you make mistakes and fear will overtake you if you allow it. Insecurity will be knocking at your door often and you will, at first, second guess many business decisions you have to make. There were many times in the beginning that I either felt sorry for myself or I felt I had made a huge mistake starting our horse business. Insecurity became a big part of my life for a short time as I started to feel like I didn't know enough to be taking care of other people's horses. The strong personalities of some of my boarders left me feeling pretty stupid even if I didn't show it on the outside. I realized later that my emotions and decisions were strongly influenced by how others behaved and acted each day at my barn. The boarders had control of my emotions and that led to extremely poor business decisions and a very unhealthy barn atmosphere.

Coming full circle

During the early years of running your horse business you will experience everything from complete joy to moments of bitterness and anger and possibly even a little resentment mixed into all of it. Somewhere in the middle you will realize the reality of your new life as an equine professional. If you hang in there long enough you will begin to experience a peace and contentment that is unbelievable. The new feelings you start to have knowing you are doing what you were meant to do in life will be incredible. That is when you will be thankful you stuck it out. It is a journey that is so worth it if you are willing to change and grow through all of it.

You may be nervous in your new role as an equine professional and self-conscious at first while you try to figure out where you fit into all of it with your clients. There will be awkward moments when you don't have an answer for a client and you might worry that you will look uneducated or inexperienced about the subject. You may feel overwhelmed many times and helpless when you couldn't fix a problem. There will be days when you feel so lonely you could cry and wonder if anyone else is going through what you are going through.

Then at some point in your business career things will start to shift and you will experience a new flood of emotions as you will start to feel yourself changing inside. Once you start to embrace your role as a barn owner, manager or any other equine profession that you have chosen, your life will change as never before. You will grow an inner strength so enduring that no one can take it from you. That awkward young businesswoman will grow and become a strong and very confident equine professional who loves her job. The days of feeling insecure about who you are and how your run your business will slowly disappear until one day they are gone!

Starting any kind of business is difficult and working with animals and their owners definitely brings greater challenges to the job. I was often tested to the limits and thought many things that I would be ashamed to ever say out loud! I am glad I never gave up even when things got tough. I am a fighter and I know you are too. I love my job now and it is truly an incredible career. I get to wake up each morning and step into my office and hear the beautiful sound of nickers waiting for me. There is nothing more gratifying than when I see those sweet eyes looking at me all the way down the barn aisle. That is when love and joy over take me and they are the best emotions of them all.

Get ready to embark on a journey you will never forget. If might be an emotional roller coaster at first but hang on because it will get easier and when things settle down you will be a much different person. My prayer is that you will turn those difficult days into learning experiences that will mold you into a balanced and well-rounded professional that can handle what life dishes out. Remember, that when it gets tough and you start to second guess why you got into this crazy horse business to begin with, hang in there. It does get so much better. Don't ever forget about the horses because after all, that is why you got into the business to begin with.

Your Personal Thoughts and Goals

1.   What are some emotions that you have already experienced with running your horse business?

2. If you could change one thing about yourself, what would it be?

Personal thoughts and goals

3. What are your emotional strengths? I know you have many because God has made you wonderfully perfect!!

~3~

Embracing Your New Role

"When you experience failure it will make your success that much sweeter. Embrace your failure as only a stepping stone to success."

It can seem very strange at times calling yourself a professional horsewoman. I never thought of myself as an equine professional when we first opened our boarding barn. Maybe inside I believed that the title should be more appropriately given to the riders you see competing in high level competitions or trainers that were giving clinics in huge venues. Maybe I thought it was more appropriate for veterinarians who had invested many years into schooling to get their degree. In those early years of running my stable I looked at every person who worked out of my barn in one way or another as a professional and I was still the same old me trying to figure out how to run my barn. I didn't realize at the time that they were also trying to figure things out in their own business as well. It is something that is not talked about very often among equine professionals.

I am not sure what I was thinking back then but overnight I became the caretaker of forty plus horses and had a huge business mortgage to pay each month. On the outside I still acted like a person running a hobby farm and the role of barn manager or should I say equine professional would not become part of my life and who I was in business for a few years. I believe there is a difference between calling yourself a barn manager and really looking at yourself as an equine professional. Calling yourself a professional in your field takes on a deeper root to who you are and eventually how you run your horse business. You are still a barn manager or horse trainer by title but once you own it deep inside as a professional, you will start to run your business differently. You will begin to feel more valued for what you do every day for the horses in your care. You will start to feel like you are really contributing to the betterment of the horse and the clients you come in contact with. That happened to me and it is a journey every person goes on that wants to make a living working with horses. I truly believe this is normal for most women that get into the horse industry in one way or another and we all arrive at the goal at different times. The truth is we all start out as beginners and we muddle our way through it emotionally for a couple of years until our confidence grows.

Equine professional to equine professional

Looking back to the beginning of when we started our business I can truly say that I didn't take myself seriously as a knowledgeable barn owner and manager. I was very insecure and that was part of the problem. I was nervous about my knowledge level and if someone asked me a question that I was not able to answer, it somehow validated to me that I was not good enough to do this job. That doesn't happen to equine professionals, right? I had it all wrong as to how I looked at being a businesswoman.

One of the biggest hurdles that I believe most women must crossover is when it comes to dealing with other professionals. This was a very difficult area for me to work through. I was a barn owner running a brand new boarding facility and I had many different equine professionals coming to my barn from all areas of the horse industry. I was constantly in communication with veterinarians, farriers, horse trainers and many other individuals. I was the new kid on the block and many of these professionals had been in the business for many years and I felt like I had to prove myself worthy of their respect. How do I get respect from a veterinarian or horse trainer if I don't have confidence in how I am doing things at my stable? I am going to be the first to say that it is a process and it takes time.

You are going to experience everything from the insecurity of being new in the business and feeling like you could never be as good or knowledgeable as other professionals to realizing that they had to start out just like you at one time. Every equine professional will have their own story and very few of them will have come from well-established horse families already in the business. Most of them will have begun their careers just like you - with only a dream.

> *Every equine professional will have their own story and very few of them will have come from well-established horse families already in the business. Most of them will have begun their careers just like you - with only a dream.*

Gaining respect from other equine professionals might take time but there is nothing wrong with paying your dues. As you earn your stripes you will gain strength, perspective and education and that only comes with time and experience. The one thing I want you to understand above all else is there is a big difference between earning respect from fellow equine professionals and being treated with no respect just because you are the new kid on the block. Don't get the two confused! Gaining respect in your chosen career choice is something we all go through but no one should ever treat you disrespectfully while you are learning along the way.

If you are managing a barn and horse business then other professionals should be treating you with respect and even be willing to offer honest advice that will help you - **not make you feel inadequate!** The best part is that down the road after you have a few years under your belt as an equine professional, someone new will come into the area and you will have a chance to pay it forward and help them. When that opportunity happens there is no better feeling in the world.

No more hobby farm

I believe many women think of themselves the way I use to think of myself. They love horses and are now making a living as barn owners, managers, trainers and so on but they haven't fully embraced their new title. It is funny because I don't remember the exact date that I considered myself worthy of the business title *"equine professional"* but I do know that it took many years to embrace it and own it. It is something that is deep inside of me and not something I expect others to address me as. It is very personal and it can only come from you – not how others think of you! I had to change from within and when those changes started to happen, my life and business started to change in a huge way. I started to feel like I was contributing to the horse industry and was part of a much larger group of people who are all in this together for the betterment of the horse. At that point I wanted to learn as much as I could to keep improving myself and my knowledge for running a barn and all the care involved with horses. It truly did change me in so many ways and it will change you too.

That is what I want for you as a businesswoman and equine professional. My goal throughout this entire book is to encourage you and have you look at yourself in a whole new way. Working with horses is an incredible career but it is also a very demanding and difficult job. It is not for the faint of heart. The person that jumps into it (like I did) will find themselves going through many emotions throughout the first couple of years because the responsibility of it all will catch you completely off guard. No one can adequately prepare you for all the challenges of working with horses and their owners but once you take yourself seriously and more importantly believe in what you are doing then your job will become much easier.

You are a professional horsewoman and you need to be proud of that title. You love horses but you can't go back to running your business like a hobby farm anymore. Things have changed and you are changing right along with them. It is time to celebrate all that you have accomplished!

You are a professional horsewoman and you need to be proud of that title. You love horses but you can't go back to running your business like a hobby farm anymore. Things have changed and you are changing right along with them. It is time to celebrate all that you have accomplished!

You will go through many changes and I am going to be honest and tell you that before you get to the good stuff you will most likely experience a lot of stress and some bad stuff. It happens to everyone that chooses to start their own business and many times in the process we lose ourselves for quite some time. When you finally do find yourself again, you will be amazed at how differently you look at everything. You will see things clearer through the eyes of a much more confident businesswoman and begin to really enjoy the ride for the first time.

Your Personal Thoughts and Goals

1. Do you look at yourself as a professional horsewoman? I want you to start writing down all the things you do for the horses in your care and the clients that have hired you. Write down everything because it all matters!

2. What are some of the areas that you need to grow and learn more in.

Your Personal Thoughts and Goals

3. What are some areas that you feel very confident in when dealing with horses and clients?

4. Who do you compare yourself to? Do you feel intimidated by any equine professionals that come to your stable? If so, why? This is a perfect time to be honest with yourself. Remember that no one will see this except for you.

~4~

Losing Yourself in Your Business

"Losing yourself once in a while is like taking a mental vacation. Remember to take a vacation every now and then but not for too long!"

Let me be the first to tell you that if you decide to start a horse business of any kind, it will overtake you if you allow it. I know this from firsthand experience. My life became crazy overnight. The days became a blur from trying to get the business going to working out the issues that were popping up every day with the horses and their owners. When I try to look back at those early years I honestly can't recall some of it.

Not only were my children very young and needing me but I was working another job outside the home to bring in extra cash. Our boarding business was having so many issues in many different areas that I pretty much dropped off the face of the earth to my friends and family outside of the business. I worked every waking hour trying to make our barn better and changes were a constant during those first couple of years. People were coming and going and horses were changing right along with them.

I completely lost myself in my business and that meant that everything else I was involved in outside the barn stopped. My husband David and I had been in a bible study with other couples for as long as I can remember and that was the first thing to go. Second were my friendships outside the barn. I had two very close girlfriends that I did so much with and eventually we lost touch with each other. I am embarrassed to say that I even missed the arrival of my closest friend's baby boy. His delivery had complications and I was never around for support or basically anything else. I was too busy and too exhausted every day to even visit her in the hospital. I am going to be very honest and tell you that it was truly one of the darkest periods in my life.

The wonderful news about my dear friends is that they are very forgiving of me and my absence from life outside the barn during that period of time. It finally hit me around the sixth year of our business that life was too short and I really needed to reconnect with the people that are the most important to me. I feel blessed because I had a second chance to make things right with my girlfriends but sadly there are women out there that don't get a second chance to make things right because the hurt feelings run too deep.

If I can give any bit of advice about this part of your life and horse business, don't let the business consume you so much that you lose track of the friendships that mean the most to you. If you are not careful, one day you will wake up and realize you are all alone and you will wonder how that happened. Having a horse business is great but it is not worth losing all that you love in the process.

We never see each other

It wasn't just my girlfriends that I stopped getting together with. It was also my husband. It is so strange to think about it this way but David and I worked together every day of the year but we really didn't see each other. It seems hard to imagine but it is very easy to let happen if you are not careful. We rarely talked about anything but the business and I was too tired to spend any quality time with him. We would do chores together every morning and we were by each other in the physical sense but mentally I had checked out and we both felt like we were just business partners and that was it. Everything else was missing. I didn't realize how this business and our schedules were hurting our marriage and now years later, I can see how easily it happens to many couples.

A while back I had a woman email me and ask if I would write a blog post about how starting a horse boarding business can ruin your marriage! My heart broke for this woman and I completely understood what she was going through. She was in year two of her boarding business and it was already causing so much stress on both her and her husband. She felt like giving up and her husband had already started to check out mentally. She shared with me how they were fighting about everything and the problems from the business followed right into their home. They were exhausted all the time and on top of it they had two little kids to raise. It sounded so familiar. Oh how the feelings started to flood my mind as I read her email. She had the same dream I did many years ago of building a beautiful barn and boarding horses. Her perfect dream and life were falling apart and she had no idea how to fix it.

As I wrote back to this woman I shared with her that David and I needed to get outside help for guidance and direction so our marriage didn't fall apart. It was truly the best thing we did for ourselves and it helped set the foundation for learning to own and run a business together. I now believe that is it something that every couple should do together if they are going to start a business and work together in all areas of the business. Even if you have a rock-solid marriage when you start your business it will be tested beyond the limits in unexpected ways. Talking with someone outside will give you a fresh perspective and allow you to voice your feelings in a safe place.

No one can prepare you for the emotions that can come with starting a business and those emotions will deeply affect your relationships if you are not aware of the signs.

Don't lose yourself completely

I want you to know that there is a light at the end of the tunnel. As a woman, wife, mother and friend I needed to find a balance in my life and separate the business from my personal life. This is vital for anyone going into business and the sad truth is that I believe many women don't realize this until relationships have been hurt.

We have this false idea that if we work harder, then the business will do much better faster. Well, yes it does take hard work but all that hard work doesn't mean much if your marriage is falling apart or you've missed your children growing up. It doesn't mean squat if your closest friends are long gone and you have no one to call when you need someone to talk to.

I am one of the lucky ones! After many years of dropping off the face of the earth because of our horse boarding business, I was able to rekindle my friendships with my girlfriends. I was also able to rekindle the closeness with my husband and our marriage is stronger than ever. I believe this journey we both went through has taught us so much about what is truly important and now we are going on almost thirty years of marriage! We returned to a bible study once a week with friends and it was like we never left. I started finding myself again apart from the business and that has rejuvenated me for when I am working in the barn. It has made me a much better businesswoman and a much happier person.

I truly believe that when you have a healthy balance between work and your private life with family and friends it will overflow into your horse business and it will show. Your clients will notice a happy and healthier you and so will your friends and family. Today I encourage you do some soul searching in this area and reconnect with the people who mean the most to you.

I still love my job more than anything and being around the horses and the people that come to our barn is a joy. I also know now that I don't need to be in the barn twenty-four hours a day. I can set boundaries and it is okay. Finding yourself again is a journey that leads to a healthy balance, empowerment and success in your personal and professional life.

> *Finding yourself again is a journey that leads to a healthy balance, empowerment and success in your personal and professional life!*

Today I encourage you to keep a little bit of yourself free to make lunch dates with your girlfriends and date nights with your husband. You can join a book club or take an art class. Think about other things that you are passionate about and try them. Even if it is only a couple of times a month those hours will be very beneficial to your well-being. The barn will be there and the horses and your clients will be fine. You might find out that many of your clients will be truly happy for you and that you are finally taking some time out for yourself.

It is true that starting a new business will take up much more of your time than you ever imagined. It does take hard work and with horses the work really never stops. Today I want you to be in control of your business and personal life so that you don't lose what is most important to you.

Your Personal Thoughts and Goals

1. What are some things you have given up since you started your horse business?

2. Do you feel like you are in control of how much time you spend with the horses, clients and chores? If you don't, then start making a list of the things you can do to change that. It might mean simplifying chores or downsizing horses and clients.

Your Personal Thought and Goals

3. Write down a list of the things you love to do outside the barn and business. It could be having coffee or lunch with a girlfriend or reading a good book. Take time to ride your favorite horse on a long trail ride!

After you have made your list of things you love to do outside the barn, make it a goal to do a couple of those things twice a month. The most important thing is to make sure it is away from the stable and business and if you can get off of the property that is even better. Remember it is baby steps. Only then will you will start to clear your mind, relax and start to find yourself again and that is extremely important!

~5~

When Did I Become So Crabby?

"Allowing others to define who you are will only lead to unhappiness. Being true to yourself and all that encompasses your heart will lead to beautiful contentment and a joy no one can take away"

I am smiling as I am sitting here at my computer because I know to some of my boarders I probably appear to be crabby quite often. Especially the teenagers! I had always considered myself an easy-going person until we started our horse boarding business. It's okay to laugh out loud because I am as I'am writing this! It truly does change you in ways that you can't imagine and for many different reasons.

Figuring out how, when or why I became so crabby (or at least how it feels at times) is something that I believe many women ask themselves as they grow with their business. Could I blame it on my age and hot flashes? Sure I guess that would be an easy excuse but seriously probably not. Could I blame it on the fact that it is extremely hard to watch a place that you have built with sweat and tears slowly start to wear out? That would be more like it. It might be that watching certain clients treat your barn and amenities with little or no respect and even at times are very hurtful towards their horses and fellow equestrians. Finding the reasons that you have become crabby at times definitely involves a little soul searching. At least it did for me.

Don't let the bad attitude linger

Women can be highly emotional and we tend to keep mental notes of everything and I mean everything! At times we may forgive but we truly don't forget. It lingers with us and as an equine professional you will find yourself having many mental discussions about the things you see and what upsets you. I still have these discussions with myself once in a while but, thank goodness, not as often anymore. I have found that women tend to keep checks and balances where men just let it go and move on. It is over and done with for them and I wish it was as easy for us women.

As a barn owner you are going to contend with this part of being a professional often. The reason is that people are people and your clients are going to do things that will either upset you (if you allow it) or annoy you because it is different than how you would do it. You need to stop and breathe if you feel this coming on. It may be your barn but your clients should have the freedom to do things the way they would like with their horse as long as it falls within the rules of your barn or stable. It is something that can be a real struggle and learning to separate our personal feelings and opinions from a situation is a process and it can take time.

I want to encourage you to throw away the habit of checks and balances that most of us do. Remember that even if you had a very bad experience with a client that doesn't mean all your clients are bad. If you take the time to find out why something is happening before you become upset you might realize very quickly that it was an honest mistake. It happens to all of us at one time or another. Try never to miss out on an opportunity to create a positive ending to any situation.

Micromanaging will always cause you stress

I believe one of the reasons we as women become short tempered and annoyed is because we try to micromanage what our clients are doing. If you are micromanaging your clients then the best thing you can do for you and your business is to **STOP**. Your clients need to learn and grow and that is very difficult if you are constantly telling them how to do things especially with their horse. Sure, it may not be the way you would do it but if you give them a chance to learn on their own, their horsemanship will improve right along with them. I have seen some wonderful things happen when a person can learn and grow in a safe environment where there is no fear of being laughed at or criticized.

As a professional horsewoman you need to learn when to encourage, educate and even have heart to heart talks when rules are not being followed and safety is compromised. Many of the things that clients will do are between them and their horse and involving our opinion is not always appropriate. If you can let some of the small stuff go you will find yourself with more time to get other things done and even time for yourself. It is mentally better for you and once you start to relax you will feel a weight lifted off of your shoulders. Micromanaging has no positive purpose and the results often lead to hurt feelings or clients who leave for another stable.

To some of my clients, especially the teenagers, I probably seem like the crabby barn owner at times. I am the enforcer when the rules are not being followed because no one else is going to say anything. And they shouldn't have to. It is my job as the barn owner and manager. I am the one that needs to remind the kids about safety and cleaning up after themselves in the barn. It will seem constant at times and depending on the day and how tired you are you might come across as stern or crabby. Your clients don't realize or care that your day started very early and on many days you don't quit until late in the evening.

As a professional I have had to work very hard in this area and think before I speak. I have learned over the years that talking with teenagers is going to be different than reminding an adult to clean up after themselves or to turn off the lights. You can't control how a teenager is going to respond after you talk with them but you can control how you handle the conversation. The interesting thing is that no matter how gently you say it they sometimes still feel like they have just been yelled at. I understand this first hand because I have two teenagers and it happens in my own home. You have to let that go and not worry about it. In many cases this is when I call the parent just to make sure things don't get skewed along the way.

You will find yourself practicing speeches on how you are going to say things to someone at your stable when the conversation is going to be a hard one. I have done this many times throughout the years but it does become much easier. After many trials and errors on what to say and what not to say, you will learn what works for you and what you feel comfortable with. Sometimes you just need to spit it out and move forward!! I have always found that praying before I have a difficult conversation with a client always takes some of the stress off of me and it calms the nerves. Also remember "practice makes perfect" and you will get lots of practice!

Becoming less tolerant is okay

I have definitely changed over the years as a businesswoman. I am less tolerant but have more patience at the same time. Is that possible? I believe it is. I have learned to be slow to speak when something is upsetting me and to really think about how I want to say it before I blurt it out. I also don't have time anymore for people who flat out don't want to follow the rules or have respect for my barn, property and especially other people at the barn. It is all part of growing as a businesswoman and it is a much needed part of becoming whole as an equine professional.

> ***There is a huge difference between being less tolerant and being crabby***

There is a huge difference between being less tolerant and being crabby. You can't control how your clients will perceive you and you need to be okay with some of them thinking you are crabby at times. Reminding your clients of rules around the barn will become part of your job and it is as simple as that. Sending out reminders doesn't make you a crabby person, it makes you a business owner that wants to keep her barn running smoothly and in good condition. Remember you are in it for the long haul.

I believe that when you get to the point that you don't worry as often about what your clients think of you, your job will become easier when dealing with uncomfortable conversations. You will also gain a greater respect for the wonderful boarders you do have and they will gain a new respect for you. Mutual respect and growth in a business comes with many steps forward and a few steps back. Get ready because you are going to learn a great deal about yourself as you continue on this incredible journey as a professional horsewoman.

Your Personal Thoughts and Goals

1. How would your clients perceive you today? How do you see yourself? Are you an easy going person or tend to be intense and at times short-tempered?

2.   Think about some difficult conversations you have had with clients and write down some things you would do differently if you could have that same conversation again. This was a great exercise for me because I blew it many times during the first couple years of business.

Your Personal Thoughts and Goals

3. Start making a list of positive words you can use when speaking to someone that will help end a challenging conversation on a positive note. This exercise really does work! Remember it is all about your tone and the words you use that can change the direction of how a conversation is going to end.

~6~

Money and Your Business

"Most people never get rich working in the horse industry but they are rich beyond their dreams because they are doing what they love."

It is very true when they say that most new businesses start off broke. It is even truer when they say that many new businesses go under during the first five years. The financial pressure is huge and the adjustment you will go through is even greater if you were accustomed to having some of the finer things in life. This change in finances can take its toll on anyone and it sure did for me especially in the early years.

The carefree life David and I had before we started our business was not noteworthy but we did enjoy a little travel and time off to do things with our children. We were a middle-income family and lived a pretty simple life. The stress of not being able to pay our bills or buy food was not something I needed to worry about. Then we opened Vinland Stables.

Things changed overnight

Once we signed the business loan papers and drove home my head was spinning and I have to admit I was in complete shock at what David and I had just done. We had become business owners overnight but we didn't have any business experience at all. The bank had loaned us an enormous amount of money to build a huge barn and indoor riding arena and purchase whatever else we needed. It was crazy to say the least!

We were up and running and into our second year of boarding horses and I was feeling the full effects of what it meant to have a business and a large loan attached to it. We were broke. We had problems with our builder which ended up in a lawsuit and in the end we needed to borrow a lot more money just to finish the barn. After we were in full operation it seemed like we were always short of money and we were quickly realizing how much we needed to fix around the farm to accommodate forty horses. Then there was the hay and bedding. Wow do forty horses eat a lot of hay!! It took us over two years through all four seasons to get a real feel for how much it would cost on a monthly basis to keep the barn in operation.

My life changed overnight and it wasn't just about the chores or working seven days a week. It was also very much about the lack of money after most of the bills had been paid. I started to feel a financial heaviness each month and I also had two little girls who I wanted to buy things for like most moms. I was very excited about our boarding business but often became very unhappy about the things I couldn't financially provide for my family. Here I was with this beautiful barn and I couldn't afford to buy some of the simplest things my girls needed. Budgeting became a way of life and that meant doing without in a huge way. It became emotionally draining for me.

Early on I resented the fact that I had to budget so tightly and at times I became angry. I blamed the builders for our financial situation and there were times I just wanted to have a pity party during those early years. It wasn't until a few years later that I started to take responsibility for what happened to us and that is when things started to change for the better. I had to put my big girl panties on and make things happen for the sake of our family. Together David and I started to dig in for the long haul and focus on getting out of debt. Once we changed our focus from playing the victim to taking control with a game plan, things emotionally got better for us. We moved forward without looking back.

> *Once we changed our focus from playing the victim to taking control with a game plan, things emotionally got better for us.*

Starting with me

Once I finally accepted our financial situation for what it was I needed to make some big changes. We were broke even though we had a full barn and income was coming in each month. The bills were so large that we were barely making it. If we were going to pay off some of the extra debt we had acquired then I was going to have to live a different way. Our life (my life!) was going to change forever in more ways than one.

Changing my spending habits was something I thought I was ready to do emotionally and I soon developed a financial game plan that I worked on every day but I will be the first to admit that is was much harder than I expected at first. I would become weak and rebel and that is when I would go out and spend money we didn't have! I never spent excessively where it would set us back too much financially but it didn't help the situation either. We were not getting anywhere very fast and at times I was slowing down the process because I was having mini money tantrums! It was extremely emotional for me at first and I had to learn how to take the emotion out of it. When I could do that, I started to feel like things were going to be okay.

Now many years later I have the privilege of talking with women from all over the country and when we talk about their barn and business the finances almost always come up. It is such a major part of any business and let's face it, without enough income to pay the bills the business will spiral downward very fast. This is an extremely difficult part of owning a business and it affects women in many different ways.

Going without is something that most women have experienced from time to time but many women will put an emotional attachment to the things they purchase. Buying can give us a feeling of temporary happiness and lifts us up. We feel better about ourselves and life and it may even give us a false sense of success about our horse business. After all, if we can afford a new horse, saddle or even horse trailer then we must be doing okay, right? I have gone down that road during the very beginning of our business and I can share with you from experience that it will leave you empty and even more financially strained if you are not careful.

> *One of the most challenging areas a woman will go through as a business owner is learning to be okay with going without.*

Your clients and money

One of the most challenging areas a woman will go through as a business owner is learning to be okay with *going without.* This is especially true in the horse world. After all horses are luxuries and maintaining them is very expensive. This means that many of your clients will have good jobs with a good income attached to it. You will watch your clients buy new horses, saddles and the finest tack. You will see them drive in with new trucks and trailers and all the fun stuff that goes with it. You will find yourself asking questions along the way. What am I doing wrong that I can't afford that? Should we just borrow the money so I can get a new trailer? Do I look unprofessional driving this old truck? And the list will go on and on and absolutely crazy questions will pop in your head.

Now I am not here to tell you how to run your finances for your barn and business. This book is not about finances at all. It is about how we as women view ourselves when times get tough and how to draw on inner strength to achieve the goals in place for our family and business.

It is about not defining who we are by the stuff we own but by how we run our business as professional horsewomen. The truth is that you can easily take out a loan and buy a new truck and trailer or even a new horse if that is what you want to do. But you need to remember that you are now a business owner and the more debt you incur will only put more pressure on you and your family for even a longer period of time.

Learning to feel comfortable with who you are while saying no to spending is a journey that will involve some serious soul searching. It is so funny because over the last fifteen years all I ever wanted was a nice horse trailer. I have looked at every model and design made and I dreamed of a three-horse gooseneck with a truck to pull it. Oh, and don't forget the large dressing room! You know we never did buy a horse trailer of any kind. I have always rented one of our boarders' trailers for all the shows we went to. Now my kids are graduating high school and I am okay with not having a horse trailer. It just wasn't in the cards because we decided it was more important to get out of debt. It was very hard early on but now I am so glad that I didn't fall into the trap of succumbing to my own desires. It was emotional for me many times but worth it in the long run not to add on the extra debt. I have been so very blessed to have wonderful boarders who are kind enough to loan us a trailer when we need one. Things usually always work out even if they are not the way we envisioned.

Their grass seems greener!

One of the more challenging parts of owning my boarding barn was the fact that I was working most of the time that I was in the barn. My clients would come out to ride and for them it was time to relax and play. They boarded at my barn to enjoy their horse and it was their time away from their hectic day. There were days when I needed to remind myself of that. It is a very funny thing how the mind works. If we allow our mind to go places it shouldn't we will find ourselves feeling jealous of the lifestyles some of our clients seem to have. I believe we are good at this and we can get ourselves into trouble if we are not careful. The truth is that I wouldn't want to have their jobs or life at all. It is so true; the grass always seems greener on the other side of the fence!

If you were to sit down and have an honest talk with some of your clients, you would find out that some of them are not living the dream at all but instead have many struggles that would break your heart. In fact, to them *you* might be living the dream and many of them would love to be in your shoes working at the barn and being around horses all day. It is good to keep things in perspective and not let your mind take you to places that are unhealthy.

When envy shows its ugly head

I want to be totally transparent and tell you that there were times when I was envious of all the things some of my clients were able to purchase and on rare occasion bitterness would try to show its ugly head. I had to make sure I was very aware of my attitude and dig deep inside to find all the positives of my situation. Because money was tight year in and year out it did wear on me many times. I found that when those negative feelings starting taking over my life, I had to fire back with prayer. That is what helped me to keep going forward and keep things in perspective of what really is important in this life. When I felt the pity party starting to happen that is when I made a conscious decision to do something nice for someone else that had less than me. When I changed my attitude and heart then amazing things happened and that is when I started to see changes and growth in myself.

Is it easy? Of course not! I have had many emotional days where I wanted to cry and stay under the covers in my bed. The great thing is that horses don't allow for that kind of behavior. If you are the one taking care of them then they still need to be fed, watered and everything else that comes with having horses on your property. The business and barn kept me going and slowly I started to grow inside and with that came many positive things. I believe horses are good for the soul and they don't allow for pity parties!

I believe horses are good for the soul and they don't allow for pity parties!

The bigger picture

If I can give a little bit of advice and encouragement, don't let money define who you are. You are a professional horsewoman who has chosen a lifestyle that is wonderful but challenging in so many ways. Having your own business is a great accomplishment in itself but the truth is that for most business owners the first few years will be financially challenging.

I want you to look at the bigger picture and realize that if you sacrifice now when money is tight, it will truly pay off in the long run and you won't regret it. You will have your barn and business for many years to come. Most of your boarders will stay (hopefully for a long time) but then many of them will sell their horses and move on where life takes them. Don't get caught up in the moment. Be smart about your finances and it will truly be freeing. You will begin to find a deeper strength that defines you and who you are as a woman and equine professional.

One last thought—When you start to feel the need to spend money you don't have on stuff you don't need for your horses, stop and go back to a time before your business. Go back even further to a time when you were a young girl and horse crazy. You would have been completely over the moon to own any horse no matter the age, breed or conformation and your life would have been perfect. You would have been excited to own some tack and a saddle even if they were used and a bit worn but they were yours and paid for. You fell in love with horses plain and simple. All that other stuff is nice but when you were young you didn't need any of it, just a horse to love. Don't ever forget that feeling.

Your Personal Thoughts and Goals

1. This is a tough one but so freeing if you do it — Make a list of your financial debt and work on paying it off from smallest loan to largest. Once you start seeing some of your smaller debts disappear, you will start to feel empowered and the stuff you thought you needed, will no longer be important.

Your personal Thoughts and Goals

2. Today I encourage you to do something nice for someone in need. You might have a client that is struggling with something that you are able to help with. It doesn't need to be big or expensive but it could change a person's day. This new perspective will start to change you from the inside out in ways you never imagined.

~7~

I Don't Feel Respected In My Barn

"When you treat the people in your life with respect
even when they don't deserve it,
you will be creating an atmosphere that sets your horse business
apart from all the rest.
Don't underestimate the power of respect."

One of the most common frustrations I hear often from other barn owners and managers is that they don't feel respected by their boarders. They feel like many of their barn rules are ignored and their stable and amenities are treated with little respect. Their clients will come to ride and leave the place in a complete mess and at times things will be found broken with no one admitting they did it.

Showing no respect lends itself in many different ways and the sad truth is that you find less and less respect these days from people in all walks of life. It doesn't really matter what line of work you are in or what business you may own, you will find similar issues about care and respect a common problem in many circles. Lack of respect for a person's place or things is one thing but lack of respect aimed at you personally will be much more painful.

My barn was complete chaos during the first couple of years. After we had already been open for a while I finally put barn rules together and there were a couple of boarders with strong personalities that chose not to follow them. I had people laughing at my reminders and notes and basically doing whatever they wanted including telling other boarders what to do. It was stressful to say the least.

As the barn owner it was very difficult walking into my barn at times during the early years. There were days that I would walk in and the atmosphere would be tense and it would become extremely uncomfortable. You know that feeling when you walk into a room and people stop talking? That was the same feeling I had in my own barn.

Because I was a new barn owner I had no idea how to handle this. I knew we were having problems in our barn and I didn't know where to begin to fix it all. Like most women I can be extremely insecure at times and as a new business owner my own self-worth and confidence were definitely lacking. In fact, there were days that I would do my chores and get back in the house as soon as possible. I almost felt like I didn't belong in my own barn. In my heart I knew how to take good care of horses at our farm but I was allowing other people to tell me how I should run my barn and even feed and turnout horses. It is a terrible way to run a business and it is even worse for the barn atmosphere.

When questioning is normal

It is only natural for a new barn owner or manager to be watched closely by their clients. When you are new at your job it can be commonplace in the beginning for clients to question your knowledge and capabilities. After all they are trusting you to take good care of their horse.

There is a huge difference between questioning a person's credentials as an equine professional and how they run their barn (especially if they are new at what they do) and allowing someone else to take over the barn and influence others by discrediting or questioning with ulterior motives. These two types of questioning are on opposite sides and each have a much different outcome. The first is positive and normal and the second is very negative and can hurt a person's confidence and business. I have experienced both and I have learned to embrace the new client who questions many things at first with my goal and desire to create trust and ultimately a happy client. I have also learned to see the signs when someone is out to damage my credibility and business by putting questions of doubt into the minds of everyone they come in contact with and questioning my knowledge with an ulterior motive. I have experience this firsthand a couple times throughout my career boarding horses and it painful and very stressful when it is happening. There are many women who are equine professionals that feel this is happening to them and it will break your spirit and confidence quickly if you allow it to continue. You will also feel like you are playing defense and trying to do damage control from this type of client. If it gets to that point then it is time to have a serious talk with the person who it doing all the talking. It's not easy but it is necessary and often it is better to cut them loose from your barn as a client.

This part of the journey you are on will be difficult in the beginning and I believe every professional will experience this to some extent. I don't believe you can grow without experiencing adversity at times and you need to know you are not alone. How you choose to deal with it when it is happening is something that you will need to dig deep inside to find. We all have an inner strength just waiting to be brought out into the open. But it may not show itself until you are put to the test and forced to bring it out. Many people never dig deep enough to find that place where they start to take control of their business and that is why many of them end up quitting. Don't go there. You've got what it takes-now you need to use it!

Respect needs to start with you as the professional. Respect towards your clients, shows that you have strength, fairness and leadership without ever having to say it. You can disagree and still show respect to your clients. Respect is so valuable that without it in a business there is sure to be huge issues.

> **Respect towards your clients, shows that you have strength, fairness and leadership without ever having to say it.**

Finding your way takes time

I did a lot of soul searching during those early years to find out what my strengths and weaknesses were in how I ran my barn. I had to come to a point where I felt comfortable in my new role as a barn owner and the CEO of my business. I finally realized that I was not getting the respect I should have as a barn owner only because I was not leading and running my business as a confident businesswoman. I was choosing to let my clients make decisions and do what they wanted to do. I was allowing the drama and negativity to run through the barn like a cancer. I was even allowing others to tell me how things were going to run in my barn! The truth was that I didn't get the respect that I wanted because I was not in charge and I was not giving respect back to my boarders. Things needed to change starting with me and it was a process that didn't happen overnight. Once I accepted my role and took charge of my business, I experienced a new kind of freedom that was incredible.

I now believe it takes most women a couple years to fully grasp their new role as an equine professional. It doesn't matter whether you are boarding horses or training them for a living. You will have many different clients no matter what part of the horse industry you choose. It is a journey that takes baby steps. You will make decisions and then second guess yourself often at first but with each decision comes a seed of confidence deep inside that no one can take away from you.

In the beginning you will worry about everything regarding how your clients feel about the decisions you make on a daily basis. You will even receive many opinions about the changes you are making and the barn rules that you are now enforcing. You will feel pressure to lighten up and in the end you might even lose a few boarders. But if you stand strong you will gain a confidence that will reinforce your actions. When you start to get those little sparks of confidence and courage you will recognize it immediately. Your eyes will be opened to a new way of doing things and you will begin to look at yourself as a competent equine professional. That wonderful feeling that comes with confidence will sustain you through tough situations, will be self-reinforcing and will strengthen over time.

> *When you start to feel those little sparks of confidence and courage you will recognize it immediately. Your eyes will be opened to a new way of doing things and you will begin to look at yourself as a competent equine professional.*

The best part of all

The best part about all of this is that leadership and respect run together. Once you start to effectively lead your horse business and all that goes with it, you will find yourself earning the respect of your clients. You might not please all your clients with the new and improved you and you need to be okay with that. As you move forward you will have new boarders come to your barn or new clients in your training program who will love the fact that you are in control of your business. Your job and life will become so much easier when this starts to happen and each day will get better as you grow. Remember that if you don't lead then someone else will. It is just a fact about life and people and the same will be true for your horse business.

> **Remember that if you don't lead then someone else will. It is just a fact about life and people and the same will be true for your horse business.**

Respect is something that will come more easily when you are running your business as a confident leader. It comes when you are willing to make tough choices for the betterment of your barn and stick by your decisions. It comes when you are honest and show integrity in every part of your business. When your clients respect you as an equine professional they will trust your decisions and you will weather the storms that any business goes through.

Learn from people you respect

The one thing that is missing in the horse industry is a mentorship program to help the equine professional in their business. In most careers there are programs to help a new manager get through their first year of running their business. The same is true for teachers that are right out of college and are put in a classroom with children and many different issues to deal with.

The first couple of years of business ownership are truly the most difficult and they can make or break you if you don't have respect from your clients. That is when the job can become ten times more difficult. One of the best things you can do for yourself is to find someone to mentor you as you navigate through your first few years as a businesswoman. They will help you by sharing the struggles they went through and they should also be someone that can give you honest feedback and encouragement along the way.

Initially you are going to have many questions about running your horse business and you will question yourself and your decisions more than ever. Those are the times that you need someone to pick you up when you are feeling pushed down to the ground. You are stronger than you know and you will get through the tough issues one day at a time but it will become so much easier with someone by your side to help you work through some of the common issues that plague most new businesses.

Remember that you are not alone and every person that has ever started a horse business has gone through many of the things you are experiencing. The women that are successful are the ones who had the courage to ask questions and find help when they needed it. I wish I would have been this smart when we started our boarding business. It would have saved me a lot of pain and heartache in the beginning.

Your Personal Thoughts and Goals

1.   Do you feel respected?   Are you showing respect to your clients? Remember you can't control how they will respond to a conversation you have with them but what is more important is how you talked to them during that conversation.   Was it respectful? Only you know in your heart.   Dig deep and grow from each conversation you have with a client. You will grow more from the difficult conversations then you ever will from the easy ones! Embrace each one because they are defining moments and I can guarantee that you will remember them years down the road when a similar situation arises.

Your Personal Thoughts and Goals

2. Make a list of people you respect as leaders and learn from them. Watch how they handle adversity and read books they have written. Be a sponge and learn as much as you can from those who have been there before you.

~8~

Making Decisions as the Barn Owner or Manager

"Every decision you make for your business will only become more challenging if you are not willing to stick by them when they are easy."

One of the most challenging areas of having my new business had to do with all the decisions I needed to make regarding the barn and the horses. Now I know this shouldn't have come as a surprise for me since I had worked at barns before but it was much different when I became the barn owner. Every decision I now made would all fall back on me both good and bad and it added a new kind of pressure that I was not ready for.

As a woman I made decisions every day regarding my family and how my day was going to go. If my children or husband were not completely happy with what I chose to make for dinner it was not that big of a deal. As a wife and mother you know this is likely to happen once in a while. It was a whole other story when it came to running our business and my boarders.

There were many nights early on in our business when I would lay awake wondering if I had made the right decision about a boarder's horse or a situation that needed to be changed that would affect the barn. I would worry when we chose to keep the horses in due to inclement weather because there was always someone that had wished we put the horses out. The same would be true for the opposite. We would put the horses outside for the day and someone would say something about how they were concerned because their horse was out in the rain. When wintertime came the challenges escalated because everyone had a different idea of managing horses in the snow and cold. I had boarders that would worry that their horse was cold so they would drive over to the barn on their lunch hour and bring them inside when it was a beautiful day. There were even times when I was questioned for my decision to put the horses outside like I was causing them great stress and harm due to the weather. I knew that the horses were completely fine but it did leave me questioning my barn management skills and knowledge about horse care.

There have also been times over the years that I have had to decide when to talk to a boarder regarding an issue. I knew in my mind that the outcome might not be positive and I would sit up in my house and go over in my head how I was going to address the subject. I have had to ask a trainer to leave for the betterment of our entire barn and my business and that was truly one of the most difficult decisions and conversations I have ever had. The results of that decision led to loss of clients and a split in our barn for a short time.

Sometimes your decisions will not only affect you but it will most likely affect your clients. During those early years I took many decisions very personally and in many ways it may have clouded my decision making because I didn't want to deal with the inevitable outcome. Avoidance is not something a barn owner or equine professional have the option of taking.

I have listed only a couple specifics of issues I have had to make hard decisions about as it related to my clients but as a businesswoman you will make many decisions often (even daily) and the consequences could leave you second guessing yourself on a few of them.

Many decisions to make

These types of decisions for your barn and business are difficult and as an equine professional you are going to go through them. As women we want to please our clients but as time goes on you will start to learn that it needs to be a business first. That means that the issues you might be avoiding need to be addressed. **That is when the businesswoman inside of you needs to come out and take control!**

Everything you do regarding your business will have a decision attached to it and it will also affect your clients whether it being the horses or their owners. How you feed the horses and the type of hay and grain you offer will just be the start. You will need to decide how you want to do turnout and herd management and this area alone will come with many decisions to make and each one will affect your clients. You will decide what kind of riding disciplines you want at your barn and there will be many decisions made about the trainers that work with the horses and give lessons. You will decide what kind of barn and arena rules will work best and you will realize that making changes will be a huge part of your business especially while it is young.

What seems like a good idea when you open your barn will change more than you ever imagined over the first few years. When your barn is in full operation you will be making decisions every day based on the many special requests you will receive. You will need to decide with each request if you can provide it or not and at some point down the road you will figure out that it's okay to say no to some of them. Learning to say no will be one of the best things you will ever do for yourself, your family and your business. That is a promise!

> *Learning to say no will be one of the best things you will ever do for yourself, your family and your business.*

It is easy to compare yourself to others

One of the most crippling things we can do is to compare ourselves to other barn owners, managers, trainers or professionals in our career field. Let me be the first to say that I did this early on and I believe now that most women do this from time to time throughout their life. We do it in our personal life and we do it as professionals. There is nothing wrong with watching how another person runs their business and it can be extremely helpful to get fresh ideas from other people-only if they can improve your horse operation. BUT as women we tend to take it a step further and we compare ourselves with others without the right motives and the end result often damages our self-worth if we are not careful.

The damage happens when you start to compare yourself to another equine professional and you start to think you will never be *good enough*. Doubt starts to invade your mind and you put that person on a pedestal while pushing yourself into the ground at the same time. It happens more than you know and we do it to ourselves all the time in many areas of our life. You start to believe you will never be as knowledgeable and your barn will never be as nice and the list goes on and on. When you begin to doubt your own skills and knowledge because of your own lack of confidence that is when you start to emotionally hurt yourself. Your insecurities will become destructive to you and your business if you allow it.

If you find yourself constantly comparing yourself, your barn and your business to other professional horsewomen and businesses, take a step back and breathe. You have already done so much more than most by daring to take a chance and be your own boss. You have taken a leap of faith that you could do it and nothing worth having comes easily. Learn, grow and remember that every trainer has their own style and every boarding barn does things differently and variety is the spice of life! Set your own path and create your own style for your business. If you have come this far then you are achieving your goals and you don't need to compare yourself or your business to others unless it will help you to improve and grow as a businesswoman. If you have come this far then you are simply incredible for just trying!

You have taken a leap of faith that you could do it and nothing worth having comes easily. Learn, grow and remember that every trainer has their own style and every boarding barn does things differently and variety is the spice of life! Set your own path and create your own style for your business.

The website and social media

I am going to be the first to say that looking at other websites of boarding stables and equine businesses can be fun but it can also leave you questioning your own worth and that of your facility. Be very careful that you don't let another person's website undermine your sense of value of your barn and horse business.

Websites and social media can make anything look fabulous even when they are not. It is as simple as that. You need to remember this because when you go on Facebook and other media sites you will find that other peoples' lives seem perfect but the truth is many of them struggle just like you do. Their barn will have many of the same issues your barn is having but of course they are not going to post it on Facebook. I wouldn't either!

I encourage you to be smart when looking at other business websites. Look at them with the mindset that you want to see if you can learn something new for your barn and business and make it a positive thing. I have gained some great ideas over the years from websites and social media and some of them we use every day.

Don't over think it!

Don't over think it! This true of most women! We tend to overthink everything in life. My husband is the first to tell me when I am over thinking something. He can see it because it consumes me and everything else comes to a screeching halt. When that happens I need to stop and take a time out!

If you are at that point where your mind is constantly thinking about your barn and horse business and it is starting to consume you, stop and mentally walk away from it for a bit. It might mean going away for the weekend with your family and doing something fun and relaxing that doesn't involve horses and clients. I have found that because we live on the property where our barn is, I need to get away for a weekend or even just one day to clear my head. It is truly amazing how once you can get away from the horses, barn and your clients you will start to relax and rejuvenate. No matter what you do for a living, everyone needs to clear their head from time to time. It will do wonders for your well-being.

Making decisions will always be a part of your business and once you find out what works and doesn't work for you and your stable, you will soon be on your way to easier days. You will grow and mature more in this area than you ever dreamed and you will gain a new confidence in the decisions you make for the horses in your care. You will learn not to overthink things that are directly involved with your clients and their horses and you will gain a much more realistic view of your entire business. You will also start to think long term and the direction you want to go with your equine business. It is a natural and positive progression that is healthy for any business especially a business that is young and still changing a lot.

Today I want to give you so much credit for taking on this new role as equine professional and business owner and starting to embrace it for all that it is. You are amazing!!

Your Personal Thoughts and Goals

1. List some difficult decisions you have had to make in your business. What were some of the results of those decisions?

2. List some things you would do differently if you could as it relates to the horses and people you come in contact with.

Your Personal Thoughts and Goals

3. What great things have you learned about yourself from the hard decisions you have made for your business? Do you feel you are growing inside with each experience?

4. Name some things you would like to change about your barn, stable and business and how you do things. Name some things you absolutely love about your barn, stable and business and how you do things.

~9~

Crying Is Not a Sign of Weakness

"A strong woman is one who is able to smile this morning like she wasn't crying last night"

As I have gotten older I seem to cry at everything. Mostly good things that melt my heart but if I become mad or upset enough I will start to shed some tears. I believe many women are like this especially as they become older. It is a blessing at times and it actually feels healing to have a good cry every now and then. There have also been a couple of times during my career boarding horses that I started to tear up in front of a client during a heated discussion and I wish I wouldn't have. In fact, I have regretted it.

Myth: Businesswomen don't cry

As a businesswoman I had to figure out this emotion of crying and how it fits into my role as a barn manager especially when I was dealing with my boarders. I never expected that the early years of our business would be so emotionally challenging for me and the end results would often be tears of frustration, anger, sadness and even despair on rare occasion. I am sure if I thought about it even longer I could find many more words to express how I felt much of the time during those early years.

On the flip side there have also been many tears of joy and laughter. Between working with horses and their owners and raising my own children there always seems to be something wonderful to cry about. I am so glad that the tears of laughter and joy have definitely outnumbered the tears of anger and sadness. I am a businesswoman and I do cry but now I have learned when to cry and when to wait until I am back in my home. I believe all businesswomen cry from time to time, you just won't see it in the workplace.

The truth is that there isn't much room for crying when you are running a business, at least not in front of your clients. When you are dealing with a very stressful situation where you are in a heated discussion with an "out of control" client, crying will not help the situation at all. In fact it will make it worse most of the time. As an equine professional you are going to come across many opinions and some of them will lead to disagreements with your clients especially in the early years of your business. It almost seems like a rite of passage for new professionals to go through these conflicts and you will have some clients that will test you to see if you are strong enough and know your stuff. I wish it wasn't this way but it is a fact of life when dealing with people and the horse industry is not exempt from it.

Certain expectations

When you decide to become an equine professional and run your own business there are certain standards that you will need to maintain. How you deal with and react to tense situations with your clients is vitally important to how they will respond to you during and after the discussion is over. You need to remember that you are now running a business and just like any other business you need to be professional when dealing with the public and your clients. Crying because a discussion is not going your way or is becoming very tense and personal will set the tone that you are emotionally **NOT** in control.

Crying because a discussion is not going your way or is becoming very tense and personal will set the tone that you are emotionally NOT in control.

This can be extremely hard for those of us that naturally *wear our hearts on our sleeves* and especially if you are talking with an irate boarder who is in your face and has just called you names that you wouldn't repeat to your children. It will be even more difficult when they start to criticize how you take care of the horses and it will become very personal at that point. That is when the emotions will start to sky rocket and the tears want to flow! A few bad words thrown at you will never hurt as much as a client criticizing how you care for the horses at your stable.

I have been the recipient of criticism and harsh words and it does cut to the core. You are going to feel like you have just been stabbed in the back. It is painful for both men and women but as women we can take

85

it to another level and allow our emotions to get the better of us if we are not careful. The times that this happened to me early on in our business were painful and I had to dig deep to keep the tears from coming. You will need to find an inner strength to keep it together until you are in a place of privacy.

That is why it is so important to prepare yourself mentally before you go into a discussion with a client and the conversation has the potential to turn ugly. I have found that when I am going to talk with a client about something uncomfortable I always take it to the Lord in prayer first. This helps me to keep my focus on what is most important and it calms my nerves. It doesn't mean that the final outcome will always go as I want it to, but as long as I handle myself in a God-honoring way throughout the discussion that is what is most important to me.

I cried in the barn

I can remember the one time I cried in the barn in front of a few boarders and my farrier! I had a very heated and upsetting conversation with a boarder and she ate me up alive. I didn't know how to react and because she had an extremely strong personality she dug right into me. It was during my second year of running my barn and I was truly naïve and vulnerable about this part of being a businesswoman and barn owner.

I just assumed that if I was nice and accommodating to my boarders (basically being a YES girl all the time) then they would always be happy and have respect for how I took care of the horses and ran the barn. I was in a fantasy world all those years ago! I was so upset and hurt by this woman's harsh words that immediately after she left I sat down right in the barn aisle between the horse stalls and started crying like a baby. She had criticized me and my husband for the care we gave to the horses at our barn and I was not strong enough to stand up for myself. I crumbled. So there I was sitting on the floor crying and my farrier walked by me without saying a word. I looked at him but he never looked at me. All of a sudden this heat came over me and I found myself extremely embarrassed at how I was behaving. Suddenly it dawned on me just how unprofessional and silly I looked! I was not handling the situation the way I should have at all. I was letting my emotions take over and I looked like a pathetic barn owner and businesswoman at that moment.

To this day I always think about that time when I cried in front of my farrier. He has never said anything about that day but he has watched me grow tremendously as a barn owner, manager and businesswoman over the last thirteen years.

Don't be too hard on yourself

The one thing I want you to get out of this more than anything is that you are not alone. We have all cried at one time or another when it comes to dealing with our business and clients. If you have cried in your barn in front of your boarders, don't worry. It is not the end of the world but now it is time to look at things differently and learn to handle those extremely stressful situations in a new way. There is no avoiding confrontation from time to time with clients but you can change the outcome (at least for you) all by how you handle it. Disagreements and confrontations are going to happen but with each one will come a wealth of lessons learned and knowledge gained. Through your experiences you will become very good at keeping your emotions and tears in check.

Sometimes you need to wait

If I can give you any words of advice about this subject I truly believe that you need to address the issues at hand even when you know it is going to be difficult. Anytime you are involved in a heated conversation and your emotions are involved I want you to learn to keep close guard on them until you are done and then feel free to let it out in the privacy of your home or a place where your clients can't see you. This should only be between you and the client that is having the issues and keeping your emotions in order will help keep it that way.

It may seem like a natural thing to want sympathy and comforting words from the clients that are siding with you but it really does put them in an awkward position the longer that it goes on. They are looking at you as the barn owner and the boss of your business and with that comes a certain obligation to handle yourself in a professional manner.

Like I said earlier, I cry a lot but my days of crying over issues with clients are long gone. Learning to stay emotionally neutral can be difficult at first but it is much needed when you are running a business. The best thing you can do is to always handle each conversation in a very fair and direct way. Be honest and clear about how things are going to go at your barn and the more direct and clear you are the easier it will be to get through the conversation without falling apart.

The most important thing you need to remember is that you need to protect yourself emotionally during these times until they pass. **The longer you run your business the more you will start to embrace that it is not personal it is business.** It's very difficult at first and it is something that we all need to learn but it does happen with time and experience which you will get plenty of! When you start to feel yourself growing and changing on the inside and take yourself more seriously as a professional, you will become more confident and much better at keeping your emotions under control in the most challenging situations.

In fact one day you will wake up and go out to the barn and start working. Something will happen that needs to be addressed between you and a client and you will go on auto pilot and take care of it in a professional non-emotional way and never skip a beat. You will probably shock yourself at how well you took care of a flame that had the potential to be a fire and you will feel this new confidence on the inside and from there you will continue to flourish and lead your business in a new direction with much better results when conflicts develop.

Good times and sadness

Now on the other hand crying over the good things that happen at your barn is completely acceptable. I easily cry about the sweet things I see happening in our barn and I am not going to walk up to the house to cry tears of joy in private. If you are celebrating a huge accomplishment for someone at your barn then let them see your emotions. If the tears start to flow then let them come! It will show your clients that you care and have feelings. It will show them that your truly do care about them and their well-being and that is a good thing.

I have also cried many tears of sadness for the horses that have been put down over the years. It is never easy and I hurt for the owner of the horse just as much as if it were my horse. Share your emotions with your clients during times of sadness and hurt because those are the moments that will last in their mind and they need to see that you do care.

> *Crying is not a sign of weakness at all. It is a gift from God and it is truly good for the soul.*

I believe crying is not a sign of weakness at all. It is a gift from God and it is truly good for the soul. I just want you to think about your role as a professional and think about the situation before the waterworks turn on. There is a time and place for tears when running a business. If you are anything like me once the tears start to flow they are hard to stop!

Your Personal Thoughts and Goals

1. Are you an emotional person? Name a few things that you find yourself crying easily over.

2. Name some times that you started tearing up during a discussion and you knew it was not the right time to start crying? What did you do to correct it? How would you do it differently if you had the chance?

Your Personal Thoughts and Goals

3. List some new goals for yourself and how you handle discussions with clients. Being prepared mentally is very important going into any conversation that has the potential to turn sour. I encourage you to prepare by going over the discussion in your mind in private and remember that it is not personal, it is business. If you feel led, take it to the Lord in prayer first.

~10~

Time to Declutter Your Barn and Life!

"When you clear the physical clutter from your barn, you will quickly realize there is plenty of room for what is truly important in your business and life."

For many women the idea of taking anything to Goodwill or the local thrift store might seem like a great idea but it can take years before we actually do it. I am no exception. I have stuff in closets and the attic that I need to get rid of and for some reason I keep hanging on to much of it. I have been married almost thirty years and lived in the same home for almost that same length of time. It is remarkable how much we collect over the years. The same may be true for your barn and business.

With a boarding operation of forty horses and people coming to our place daily it would be fair to say that our barn is a pretty busy spot. Some days go pretty smoothly but then there are other days when my head is spinning from the busyness of it all.

Over the years I have acquired many things from previous boarders for many different reasons. It is fascinating how much people leave behind when they leave a barn. People have left everything from saddles and tack to blankets and even a horse trailer! My husband and I did some remodeling in our tack rooms this last spring and we found some hoof flex and very old treats from a previous boarder that had boarded at our barn eight years ago. The shelves were so cluttered with stuff that we never noticed all the items that had been left behind.

When our tack rooms were cleaned out and reorganized I absolutely loved it. It felt like it was a new beginning in a strange sort of way. All the stuff that was just laying around was gone and everything had its place. It was such a great feeling and once the tack rooms were cleaned out I wanted to keep it that way. I also believe my boarders felt the same way.

After we had cleaned out our tack rooms it inspired me to start on our lounge and bathroom area. I started making many trips to Goodwill with items I no longer wanted. The more I cleaned out the stuff that had been collecting dust over the years the more I wanted to keep going.

Getting started is the hardest part

I love to tour other barns and see how they are designed. Actually I would rather walk through a barn then go on a walk of a parade of homes any day. There is something about a horse barn that I just can't get enough of.

I have been in some very clean barns with everything in its place. I have also walked into many barns where there is stuff everywhere. I have even been in a few where you can hardly walk down the aisle or get your things out of the tack room because there is so much junk packed into every corner. When I am in a barn like that I want to start picking up the things that are laying around and start organizing. Of course I don't but oh how I want to!

> *When a barn is extremely cluttered and unorganized, you will often find out that the rest of the business and how it is run daily is cluttered and unorganized as well.*

When a barn is extremely cluttered and unorganized, you will often find out that the rest of the business and how it is run daily is cluttered and unorganized as well. It is very hard to run a horse operation smoothly when stuff is everywhere and you can't find what you need because you have too much junk all over the place. You will find that when your barn is less cluttered it will make your life and business less cluttered. They go hand in hand.

Today I want to encourage you to take some time and start getting rid of all the things that are making your job in the barn more difficult. You will be amazed at how much easier your job will become with less stuff all over the place. It will create an atmosphere that will feel calm to not only you but your clients. When everything is in its place, it tells everyone that you run a very organized business and you know what you are doing. When your place is clean and without all the clutter you will be pleasantly surprised at how this will make your job as the barn owner or manager so much less stressful.

> *When everything is in its place, it tells everyone that you run a very organized business and you know what you are doing.*

As women it is hard to let things go and that will be very true for your barn as well. As you declutter your barn and business you will also be simplifying your life. I believe we could all use some simplicity in our lives. **Don't underestimate the power of less!**

Your Personal Thoughts and Goals

1. Name some areas in your barn and business that you need to clean out and reorganize.

2. If you find yourself procrastinating because it overwhelms you, take baby steps and tackle the smallest job first.

Your Personal Thoughts and Goals

3. Keep a list of the things you have cleaned out and reorganized in your business. Even the smallest of tasks are important! Write down each one you complete and then write down two words that describe how it makes you feel inside. Your sense of accomplishment is going to grow with each completed job and it will motivate you to keep going.

~11~

Learning to Say No Is a Great Thing!

"When you say yes to your clients, make sure you are not saying no to yourself."

Learning to say no is not easy. In fact just the thought of saying no to a friend or client will involve many emotions and you will have a few personal conversations with yourself before you finally make a decision. Most women have a very hard time with this especially in their younger years. I was no exception. It is our nature to want to please others and not disappoint. We tend to carry the burden of guilt when we say no to someone we care about and then we start to worry about our relationship with that person. Our minds can even take it further if we allow it. Now carry that over into your business. Do you find yourself having trouble when it comes to saying no to your clients? If so, you are not alone at all. Most new businesswomen struggle with this

99

problem for the first few years of running their own barn or horse business.

I am going to be the first to say that I was a *yes* person when we first opened our boarding facility. I was lucky to have a full barn and I wanted to keep it that way. I worried that if I didn't say yes to all the special requests I received, soon I would lose boarders and have empty stalls. Our business mortgage was huge and the pressure to keep the stalls full, clouded my judgement much of the time during our early years of business ownership.

As women we say yes for various reasons. As an equine professional we want our clients to think we are the best thing ever. We want them to tell other horse owners what a fantastic place our barn is and that they should move their horse. We want the affirmation that we do an incredible job with the horses in our care. Unfortunately when we say yes to every request that is asked of us something is going to give. It happened to me and if you have a larger scale facility you will find out quickly that it will start to burn you out if you are not careful.

Living on the property

In many businesses the motto is *the customer is always right*. That may be true for a lot of small businesses but when you are dealing with horses the situation changes drastically. The one thing I want you to think about is the fact that for the majority of horse facilities the owners or barn managers live right on the property. They never truly get away from the work unless they go on vacation. That makes your career much more demanding in a very unique way. The horses need care seven days a week and every day of the year. There are no days off when you choose to care for horses on your property unless you can hire employees and even then you really never get away from it. Remember that whatever your employees do both good and bad will always come back to you and you are responsible for their actions. The buck stops with you as the barn owner or manager.

When this becomes your career of choice you need to find a work balance because every time someone drives into your driveway and every time you walk out of your house you are making yourself available for your clients without even realizing it. You are working every day to take care of all the horses on your property and the added requests with no break or days off from people or horses will start to add up quickly. Work fatigue happens more often than you know because in most new businesses the owners don't have the finances to hire help. Money might be extremely tight in the first few years so you will be in the barn much more than you had planned.

Saying yes when I should have said no

The reason I brought up the living arrangements of a barn owner or manager is because I want you to see the full picture of what your life will be like. It is the best job in the world but when you start to add in the many requests you will receive you will quickly realize your life has changed drastically in so many ways. You can't just get in your car and drive home each day from work anymore and you might have knocks at the door any time of day when there is a problem. Your career will definitely become a lifestyle and learning to set the boundaries will take time.

Your career will definitely become a lifestyle and learning to set the boundaries will take time.

Because I was new to the boarding world as a barn owner/manager I was eager to say yes to my clients. I had so many requests during the first couple of years and I was quickly realizing that my time was not my own anymore. I soon was in the barn from early morning to late at night and when I was in the house my phone would ring often. I didn't have a good business plan at the time to charge for extra services performed so I was doing many extra services for free and it was taking me away from my children and personal life. I had to find some direction on how I wanted to deal with all the special requests I was receiving.

There were many times early on when I would do something for a boarder (like holding their horse for a farrier) and not get paid for the extra time it took me. I started to resent this part of the job. I was working longer hours and not making a penny more. When I finally started charging for extra services or declined a request that I knew I couldn't do I started to feel a huge weight lift off my shoulders. I started to make money when I put in extra time for special requests and at the same time I began to have fewer requests. My life and barn was slowly changing in many ways and I was changing right along with it. I was making extra money and had more free time! The best of both worlds!!

I started to make money when I put in extra time for special requests and at the same time I began to have fewer requests. My life and barn was slowly changing in many ways and I was changing right along with it. I was making extra money and had more free time! The best of both worlds!!

Things were starting to become better for me but how did my boarders feel about the changes I was making? The reality is that no one wants to pay extra money for services that they thought were included in the board. It was a big change at our barn and it was part of growing as a business. When I started to say no or add an extra fee for a service preformed I was surprised that most of my boarders were supportive. I still have some clients that would prefer to pay for many extra services and I am fine with that. I also have many clients that help each other out instead of using my services and that works out great for everyone.

This change was something that I needed to do for myself and my family and I have never regretted it. I am happy to agree to reasonable requests but I have learned it is okay to say no. **This is where I want you to be. When you can say no and have no guilt (because it is not personal, it is business) you will feel the stress start to leave and you will do a better job of running your horse business because you will have a healthier balance in all of it.**

Bending the rules for a client

Another area of your business that you will find challenging at times will involve your barn rules. No matter what kind of barn rules you set up for your place you will have boarders that will ask you to change them for their own special needs. This part of the job can be just as stressful even though it doesn't take up any of your time except for the time you spend explaining why your answer is no.

This was extremely hard for me during the early years of running my barn. I would have the nicest person in my barn come and ask me for special privileges that go against the barn rules and it was extremely hard to say no. In fact, I said yes many times with regret following quickly behind. It again was something that I had to experience and grow through and it took me years to stop making exceptions in this area.

This was especially difficult when I was friends with the client. Later on down the road I started to experience a new kind of emotion when I was put in this uncomfortable situation by a client. I started to experience resentment because I had been put on the spot for special privileges and requests. The resentment was greatest when my closest clients would ask me for favors that went against barn rules. I had to sort through my emotions quickly and deal with my hurt feelings. I felt at times like I was being taken advantage of by our client/friendship relationship. It was a lot to fully grasp and it made the job much more complicated.

The truth is that it will be easier to say no to some of your clients than others. This is where you need to be especially careful and treat everyone the same at all times no matter how close you are to a certain client. You can't have it both ways because it just doesn't work and it is bad for your business as well as your reputation as a business owner.

The truth is that it will be easier to say no to some of your clients than others. This is where you need to be especially careful and treat everyone the same at all times no matter how close you are to a certain client.

You will have boarders that want to stay later than your barn hours and come before your barn opens. You will be asked to make exceptions for many different reasons so they can ride, blanket or care for their horse. You will have boarders that pay late each month because they feel they can even though you have told them the board is due on the first of the month. You will have clients that will use other people's things without asking and you are going to be the one to tell them they can't do that. Even though many of the things I have listed are not direct requests, if you turn and look the other way then you are saying "yes" it is okay to do those things. That is when you need to be direct, say no and bring the issues out in the open. Address them even when you know it is going to be difficult.

You cannot bend the rules for one person because if you do then every other person will notice and your barn will start to have serious issues. You need to remember that allowing a client to bend the rules is the same thing as no rules at all and I am the first to tell you it will only cause serious problems and wear you out!

They are upset with me!

Let me start off by saying that every businesswoman worries that her clients will be upset with her at one time or another. I don't care if you are new as an equine professional or have been running your barn for five years. The fear that you have upset your clients because you said no to a request will be a part of your world during the early years of your business. And even after you have been in business for many years those same old feelings will try to creep in once in a while when you need to say no to someone that you would love to say yes to.

As women we want to please people most of the time and that will definitely spread into your business and all the decisions you need to make. Learning to feel comfortable with the answer you need to give to a client is definitely a personal journey and I would say this is normal for many women and it can take years to master. The problems happen when you let your fear of upsetting your clients cloud your judgement in decisions you make for barn and the horses in your care. I experienced this first hand a few times.

When we opened our boarding facility I had a full barn of beautiful horses to take care of and great people to see every day. I didn't see how there could be any problems with how I ran my barn and as the requests starting coming in for me to change this or that, my life became crazy overnight. I quickly was changing many things in the barn due to special requests and it didn't stop. In fact, they increased. I had boarders that wanted everything from lights in their stalls to special paddock choices for their horses. I had boarders that wanted me to change our barn hours and how we did chores. I had a request to pile the bedding a certain way for one client because she said her horse liked it better! The requests were endless and I was starting to feel the exhaustion setting in because I was working extremely long hours and every request I said yes to made my job harder and longer at times. After all, isn't the customer always right?

I am here to say that the customer is not always right! As a businesswoman you really need to figure out what you can and cannot offer to your clients and you need to learn to be okay with your decision when your answer is no.

The customer is not always right! As a businesswoman you really need to figure out what you can and cannot offer to your clients and you need to learn to be okay with your decision when your answer is no.

Is it hard to say no? Of course it is, especially at first. You will panic a little bit inside because you will immediately wonder if they are upset with you. You will try to read the expression on their face to see if they are angry or disappointed. There will be many times early on in your business where you will second guess your decision but you need to stand strong. This is where your life as an equine professional will start to change and grow. You are going to come to a point where you realize you can't do it all and that is when you need to stop and take a good long look at your business. When you start to grow as a businesswoman and can say no when you can't offer what your client is asking for, it will change you in so many ways and all for the better.

You are going to experience many different reactions to your response when you tell a client no. You will have some clients that will become upset and even threaten to leave your barn. When this happens you need to stand strong. If they do leave then they really weren't happy to begin with and it is far better to let them go. Every time I have lost a boarder over something that I was not able to provide, a new client came that was a better fit for our barn. You will have some clients that will show disappointment and it will tug on your heartstrings but you need to remember it is a business. Above all else you will have many clients that will be very understanding of your decision. And for every no you have to say to a client, you will have far more times you can say yes and it will be awesome!!

Growing as an equine professional

You are going to grow as an equine professional and with that will come a confidence as you make daily decisions. You will be happy to say yes when you can but you will be fine with saying no when you need to. It is something that doesn't happen in the first month. It is a journey that each of us will take and you will arrive at where you feel comfortable and confident in running your business in your own timeframe.

Learning to say no is something that I believe is good for all women to do in our personal as well as professional life. We stretch ourselves too thin and the only one we are hurting is ourselves and our family. It can affect our health and in the long run it can hurt your business. The best thing you can do is to take a deep breath and think about your response before you blurt it out for a client. You will learn many lessons from the challenges you will experience and the best classroom is your barn and managing it daily.

> *Learning to say no is something that I believe is good for all women to do in our personal as well as professional life. We stretch ourselves too thin and the only one we are hurting is ourselves and our family.*

Today I encourage you to take a good look at your life and your business. If you are afraid to say no to the requests you receive and your personal and business life has become extremely stressful then there is a very good chance you are overdoing all of it. It is time to get your life back in order and that means saying no when you need to. You will never regret it.

Once you learn to say no it will change your entire life in positive ways and you will realize that your equine business will be just fine. Your clients will still be there and life will go on. Learning to say no is a clear sign that you are maturing into a confident businesswoman and equine professional.

Your Personal Thoughts and Goals

1. Name some requests that you should have said no to but you said yes instead and later regretted it. Be specific and write down what you were feeling at the time.

2. How have the special requests you have said yes to affected your personal life and family. Be specific because only then will you start to see the complete picture of why this is so important.

Your Personal Thoughts and Goals

3. Make a list of things you can offer at your barn or stable as extra services. Once you have your list, start to think about the fees that would be associated with each service. Remember that this list will change as you grow as a businesswoman. It may start out very short but it will grow as you grow and it will be okay.

~12~

They Don't Really Know Me

"Believe in who you are and not who people think you are. Live each day in a way that is honest and true to who you really are deep inside and with that will come a peace that no one can ever take away."

I have had the pleasure of talking with many women from all over the world. In each conversation I quickly realized that these horsewomen and professionals are going through many of the same struggles I have experienced with my business. They each had a dream and dove right in. Life quickly became complicated and even ugly at times for many of these women. They feel misunderstood in many ways by their family, friends and clients. This is a part of becoming an equine professional that is extremely difficult at times. On the outside things look grand but on the inside there is a woman struggling to keep her business going without it ruining her personal life. Professional horsewomen are often misjudged about who they really are.

Look at the size of that barn!

The first obvious misconception that many people believe is that if you are working with horses for a living then you must be making a lot of money. When David and I built our barn and indoor arena I never realized how differently people would look at our lives and the business we started. I can't tell you how many times I have had people say to us, "You guys must be making a ton of money with all the horses on your property." If you are boarding horses then there is a good chance that you have heard this comment. We have a large barn and arena and people will drive into our place and assume we are financially well off. What they don't realize is that with a huge barn and many horses stabled inside comes a business mortgage and high overhead to keep it all up and going. What they don't understand is that it cost a lot of money to feed all the horses and after all the bills are paid there really isn't much left. It is a misconception that many equine professionals experience and it can be very frustrating at times.

Another misconception that is frustrating is when people think running a horse business is easy. Most people don't understand the amount of work that is involved in the daily care of horses and clients. You will have clients as well as family that think you are on *vacation* every day because you are at home *playing* with the horses. Now this isn't the case with everyone but most people will not realize everything that your job demands of you physically and mentally each and every day.

Wealth and prosperity has always been associated with horses and the people who own them but for most people who love horses this is just not the case. This would include barn owners as well as horse owners.

Many of these people are just trying to make their dreams come true on a budget and sometimes that budget is very tight!

Finding Peace

Finding your peace in how others view your life and job is something that you will need to work through and be content with. As your friends and family begin to see your life become one with your business and how much time it takes you away from other things, they may start to understand that you do work a lot. They will begin to notice that you rarely go on vacation and family functions always seem to be cut short because chores need to get done. But don't be discouraged or frustrated if they don't ever get it. It is a very unique lifestyle and career you have chosen and you can't expect someone to fully understand it if they have never done it.

Today I want to encourage you not to be too hard on your friends and family. To be honest, I didn't have a real grasp of how much work it took to keep our boarding facility operating until we were doing it seven days a week every day of the year. I don't believe anyone truly gets it until they are living it themselves. Yes it might be frustrating when you hear some of the comments that people will say but don't take it personally or hang on to it. Just move forward and if you can, educate them a little along the way when the opportunity presents itself.

People come with many opinions about everything and at the end of the day it doesn't matter what they think. What is more important is that you are doing what you have wanted and worked so hard to achieve. Don't be overly sensitive to the comments you receive now and then. As women it can be hard to ignore negative comments but it will become easier the longer you are running your business.

It's okay not to have all the answers!

When we first opened our barn I worried that I might be asked questions that I couldn't answer when it came to an illness or injury of a horse in my care. I had a fear that I was going to look like an idiot if I didn't have a good answer about feeding or care or basically anything else that had to do with horses. I was in this new role as a barn owner and manager and the last thing I wanted to do was look incompetent in front of my clients.

This is a very real fear that most women go through in the beginning of their career. The same would be true for any professional in any career choice. We don't want to look incompetent and sometimes we make big mistakes trying not to look incompetent!

We don't want to look incompetent and sometimes we make big mistakes trying not to look incompetent!

As a barn owner caring for other people's horses you have the responsibility to keep current on equine care. You should have a sound knowledge of horse care if you are going to take care of horses but you shouldn't put pressure on yourself to know everything. That is impossible and yet as women we will often expect that of ourselves.

Your clients will assume because you are running a barn or training horses that you are knowledgeable about horse care and you should be. **I want to be very clear here and say that sound knowledge of horse care is important but it is okay not to have all the answers.** I have finally learned over the years that it is far better to be honest and tell my boarders that I don't know the answer but we will find out together than to act like I know what is going on and make a huge mistake. I have seen this happen many times over the years especially when it comes to lameness and illness issues. I have even seen it happen when it comes to trainers and their training program. Why is it so hard for women (or men) to simply say they don't have an answer at the moment? I have watched farriers make a hoof issue worse because they acted like they knew it all and down the road we find out they actually caused more damage.

After many years of boarding horses I still see things occasionally that I have never seen before and it leaves me stumped. The best part about it now is I don't have any problem telling my boarders that I don't know the answer. At that point we can work together to find out what is going on with the horse. In the long run of your business and career I believe you will look more professional when you are honest with your clients and are willing to grow and learn from each situation that comes up.

The next time a client shows you something on their horse and you don't have any idea what it is, be honest with them and that will impress them more then you can imagine. You will both learn together and that will mold you into a great equine professional not just by what you know but also by who you are and how you handle the things you don't know.

> *You will both learn together and that will mold you into a great equine professional not just by what you know but also by who you are and how you handle the things you don't know.*

Equine professionals are often misjudged for many reasons. It is definitely not the normal career choice for most people and it is okay if your clients and family don't fully understand what you do all day. You are going to hear different comments from people throughout your career and you will learn to let it roll off and not take is personally. Just remember that for every critical or sarcastic comment you receive, you will receive many wonderful words of support. Don't let that one negative comment ruin your day.

What matters most is that you are doing what you absolutely love and you are helping others achieve their dreams by giving lessons or taking care of their horses at your barn. You took a chance and you followed your dream and made it a reality. You are an amazing woman and equine professional and give so much to the horse industry. Don't ever underestimate what you do daily for the horses in your care.

Your Personal Thoughts and Goals

1. *How do you think others perceive you and what you do for a living? Do your family and friends understand your lifestyle? Do you have a good support system at home?*

2. *What are your favorite subjects when it comes to the overall care of the horse? For example – Nutrition, herd management. How can you grow in your knowledge on these subjects? Example-College classes, seminars, workshops.*

Your Personal Thoughts and Goals

3. *Make a list of subjects you want to learn more about regarding daily care, nutrition and medical care for the horses you will be taking care of daily. Remember that the learning never stops and we shouldn't either.*

~13~

How Did I Get So Dirty?

*"A horsewoman who is scared to get dirty shouldn't ever own
a horse but a horsewoman who can find beauty in mud
is truly exceptional because she knows the mud is only on the
surface and what lies beneath is gold."*

As I was writing this chapter I didn't envision that I was going to experience some deeper feelings about myself and being a woman but I sure did. Let's face it; if you choose to work in the horse world and hang out at barns you are going to get dirty. And I mean really dirty at times!

Beauty is something that we are definitely obsessed with. You see it in magazines or television and all over the internet. Even when you look at horse magazines the women look beautiful while they are pushing a wheelbarrow or leading a horse. Their make-up is perfect and they look like they walked out of a hair salon.

Okay so it's time to get real and find out what true beauty is all about and for each of us it will be a little different. Where we draw our strength and self-confidence is where we will find our freedom to feel beautiful even when we have old jeans on that are covered in mud and without a lick of make-up on.

> **Where we draw our strength and self-confidence is where we will find our freedom to feel beautiful even when we have old jeans on that are covered in mud and without a lick of make-up on.**

Trying to feel pretty again

I was born in Los Angeles California in the San Fernando Valley. I grew up during the seventies and eighties with big hair and pumps. It was a great time to grow up. I also had horses and rode and I often felt like I was living two separate lives. I put on jeans and cowboy boots to ride and then I would go to high school in dresses and pumps. There wasn't Facebook back then so I only had a small number of friends that liked horses and my world was very small. We had a lot of fun but as a teenager I was trying to figure out what beauty meant to me. I was awkward like many teenage girls and wore clothes that I should never have worn because I was trying to fit in. The only time I really felt comfortable was when I had my jeans on. As I grew a little older I started wearing high heels any chance that I could. I was working all the time but I dressed like I was going out to a nightclub. Fashion became part of my life for a short while. You would never know it now if you saw me at our horse farm.

Working with horses is definitely a job that takes a strong woman both physically and mentally. When you are running a barn I can promise you that there will be days when you never had time to put make-up on. Your jeans might have been worn a couple days in a row (okay let's be honest! Maybe those jeans haven't been washed in almost a week!!) with leftover mud on them from the previous days and it will be difficult to recognize what kind of boots you are wearing because of all the dirt, mud and manure that adorns them. Over time your hands will show the wear and tear of your occupation and they will become dry and weathered. You will look like the hired hand rather than the barn owner or horse trainer many days and you will feel like it often.

Some of your clients on the other hand will come out to ride and they will wear the latest in riding apparel. Their boots will be one pair of many and you will wish secretly that you could wear a pair like theirs to work even though you know it is not practical for doing chores. They will have make-up on and their hair will look perfect. You will want to run in the house and quickly put your make-up on (which I have done a couple of times – just being honest!) and fix your hair and even maybe put a nice clean pair of jeans on. You will want to look like the equestrian ready for a ride instead of the hired help ready to feed and bring horses in. It is definitely something that you mentally need to be ready for and it is a special journey every woman takes.

Defining what makes us feel beautiful is something that every woman will do throughout her life and what makes us feel pretty or even sexy will be different for all of us. I am in my fifties now and I can get pretty dirty but even with all the dirt and mud I am comfortable in my skin and that is what makes me feel beautiful. It may not be by the world's standards of what beauty is but that doesn't matter to me anymore.

Once in a while my mind goes back to high heels and big hair and I smile. Those were great times growing up but none of them can compare to my favorite old blue jeans. When I put those old jeans on I know I am where I am supposed to be and there is no better feeling.

Do something for yourself

I want you to look deep inside on those days that you are feeling rough and unattractive and do something special for yourself to make yourself feel pretty. I truly believe that when you are doing what you love for a living then the inner beauty comes out in full force and you will look beautiful even while doing chores with hay stuck in your hair and mud on your boots and jeans.

Two special assignments

I have two assignments that I want you to do. The goal is to get you thinking about what true beauty means to you. The first assignment is this:

I want you to think about all the professional horsewomen you have watched over the years and pick out the ones that you truly believe are beautiful on the inside and out. Look at their careers and where they came from and study what they have accomplished throughout the years.

When you start to learn about some of these remarkable women who have made a career in the horse industry, define what makes them beautiful to you. Read as much as you can about how they got started and all their career highs and lows as they progressed. You might be surprised to find out that many of them have put in many very long and hard days to get to where they are today. They have walked the same path you are on. They have been exhausted and worked days on end without make-up and dirt under their fingernails. They have worn dirty jeans and dealt with mud on their clothes, face and boots at one time or another. It might sound extreme but if you are working with horses in the elements then you will quickly realize that I am not making this stuff up! No glamour in this job often. Some might be younger but many of these women who are successful are a little older and the beauty they possess definitely comes from the inside and it resonates on the outside. The more you get to know them the more beautiful they become especially after you hear their story and what they have gone through to get to where they are today.

I want you to think about that when you are covered in dirt and mud and haven't worn make-up in a few days and your hair is in a ponytail hidden under a baseball cap. They have been there and I am sure they still wear old jeans and get dirty now and then especially when they are home at their farm. This is one of the things that make horsewomen stunning. Find your strength and beauty from the inside and you will glow with strength and beauty on the outside.

Find your strength and beauty from the inside and you will glow with strength and beauty on the outside.

The second assignment that I want you to do is to take some time to pamper yourself every now and then. You are going to need it! You are going to be very busy with your career and it will drain you both physically and mentally at times. You need to be deliberate in taking time for yourself and getting pampered should be a part of it. For me it is getting my hair colored and washed at a salon and my favorite thing is a body massage. Sometimes just putting on some make-up will lift me up or buying a new shirt now and then to wear in the barn. We have always been very careful with our personal and business finances but every once in a while my husband knows I need to be pampered. Because I don't work in an office where I dress up every day (and stay clean all day) it's the little things that make me feel pretty and they are easy to do. You will find what lifts your spirits and makes you feel better inside and out.

Above all else I want you to remember that beauty is not defined by the world's standards. It is defined by what makes you feel beautiful and no one can take that away from you. Some of the most beautiful woman I have had the pleasure of meeting were not physically beautiful by the worlds standards but to me they were stunning! Feeling pretty is skin deep but feeling beautiful comes from within and people will notice. Don't ever forget that.

Your Personal Thoughts and Goals

1. Write down the names of a few professional women who have left an impression on you in one way or another.

2. What is one thing that stands out in each of these women? Did they have an easy life? Did it take time for them to create a successful horse business? Do you find any similarities between you and these successful women you admire? It's okay to be honest.

Your Personal Thoughts and Goals

3. When do you feel good about yourself? What are you basing those feelings on? Are they based on your circumstances, material things, clothing and accessories etc? This is where I want you to dig deep inside your soul. Remember that you are beautiful and wonderfully made and it has nothing to do with fancy boots or name brand clothing.

~14~

Trying to Figure Out the Boundaries

"Without boundaries we often find ourselves in situations that we should be slapped for!"

This is a subject that I know most women struggle with during many times in their life. This was a huge issue for me when we opened our boarding facility. I had no idea how to manage my professional life with my personal life and having clients at my home seven days a week made things much more complicated.

As women we love to talk and share our hearts and we enjoy being around other women. When my barn opened and most of my clients were women I loved every minute of it. I would walk out to the barn and we would talk about our horses, families and every other subject imaginable. We are good at it and most women enjoy talking about pretty much anything.

I crossed the line

As our new boarding business was well into the first year I became close friends with a couple of boarders. I looked forward to when they came out to see their horse and I must admit I was excited when I would see their car drive up to the barn. The more we talked when they were at the barn the more intimate our conversations became until I crossed the line. I did the one thing that you should not do. I started talking about the barn and business and the issues we would have with other clients and our financial woes at the time. I am sure I made some of my past boarders uncomfortable at times when I shared personal things with them that I shouldn't have.

To add to my mistakes I would listen to my clients' complaints they had about each other and I did nothing to stop it. It wasn't just your basic complaining about barn issues, it became gossip and it started to make me feel uncomfortable. I was starting to be put in a position (that I allowed) where they wanted me to choose sides. I was the barn owner with clients but acting like a high school gossip girl. I was not being professional at all and I didn't know how to correct the situation as it was happening. Things got out of hand early on at my barn and at the time I didn't see how unhealthy this was for me or my business.

When I finally did start to realize that I was creating a very unhealthy environment for my barn and business things had already gotten too far out of hand. I had to learn fast where the boundaries were between me and my boarders and it wasn't easy. It took me a few years to really get a grasp of how I should act and when I should walk away from a conversation. This was extremely hard for me because I enjoyed being around these women and we would do things together outside the barn but I knew it was not the way to run a healthy stable and business.

Once you cross the line and put yourself into a situation that compromises the integrity of you and your business it is very hard erase what you have said and done. In my situation I shared too much personal stuff about our finances and the end result was worry from my boarders that we might close up shop. This is a very real fear that happens in many barns and stables all over.

The other situation that we can find ourselves participating in is gossip and it is a silent killer to any business. I had to learn to walk away when the conversation became gossip especially about other clients in the barn. This is something that I think many women get caught up in but as a professional you will need to learn to separate yourself when the talk turns negative. Remember you are running a business now and with that comes a responsibility to ALL your clients to be treated equally and with fairness and that would include private conversations you are a part of.

Once you start to set a higher standard of how you want your business to operate when it comes to personal discussions about others you will see a much more positive atmosphere in your barn and others will notice. It needs to start with you as the professional and you will set the tone for what type of business you will have. If you don't gossip then you will rarely hear any. If you are a gossip then you will hear it often and in the end you will be the one hurt both financially and emotionally because your business will be affected when people leave. It will also affect your barn's reputation and people will talk about the type of barn you have and atmosphere is a huge part of it. That is the simple truth.

> *If you are a gossip then you will hear it often and in the end you will be the one hurt both financially and emotionally because your business will be affected when people leave.*

When unpopular decisions are made

Another part of the scenario that makes the job challenging is that many professional horsewomen will live on the same property where the barn and horses are located. Very quickly this will become your entire world if you can't get away from it like most normal jobs. It can be extremely isolating when you work at the barn and you don't have much time to get together with other women outside your horse world.

It's only natural to want to talk with your clients and you will become close with some of them. Most equine professionals forget from time to time (including myself) that you are still running a business and decisions need to be made each day and it will affect all your clients. You will find yourself in uncomfortable waters if one of your close client/friends is not happy with your decisions. It will become personal at that point. When this happens it can affect the friendship and feelings will get hurt. When your business becomes too entwined with friendships it can cause a lot of stress on relationships when you need to start making decisions and acting like the professional you are supposed to be. It becomes a very clear reminder to your clients that it is a business first and for some this will cause the friendship to unravel.

This can and will become very painful if you are not mentally and emotionally prepared for this. Many business relationships are not strong enough to weather changes and often feelings get hurt for everyone involved. It took me many years to navigate through this part of my business and dealing with relationships and I still believe it is one of the most challenging parts of my job.

> *When your business becomes too entwined with friendships it can cause a lot of stress on relationships when you need to start making decisions and acting like the professional you are supposed to be.*

You are better than this and today I want to encourage you to turn the negative talk in your barn or stable into positive talk and watch the whole atmosphere change. When you start to create a safe place for your clients both physically and emotionally, your business will flourish like never before and others outside the barn will notice also. Your relationships with the women in your barn will change and grow in a new positive way with respect for each other as one of the beautiful results.

Finding a healthy balance

Finding a balance between your personal life and business life is tough but learning to find a balance between friendship and clients will feel extremely challenging many times throughout your career. This is a part of the journey that all businesswomen experience. Learning what boundaries work well for you and your business will change along the way. The longer you are in business for yourself the more defined your boundaries will become and your clients will start to recognize them as well. Let me tell you it is not easy and there will be times when you feel very lonely especially as you start to distance yourself from certain situations and conversations that are going on.

> *The longer you are in business for yourself the more defined your boundaries will become and your clients will start to recognize them as well.*

Learning to be discreet with what you share with your clients is vitally important and can be challenging for many women. It has taken me many years to grow and learn from my mistakes but I have learned to be careful. Not only is it better for my business but it is better for me.

You need to remember that at the end of the day they are still a client paying you for a service and you still have a business to run. When you share things with them about other clients it will automatically make them feel uncomfortable (some more than others) and put them in the middle of something they should not be in. I can promise you that it never turns out good. The truth is that gossip has no place in any barn or anywhere. I still have to remind myself once in a while when I get caught up in a conversation that is turning into a gossip circle.

But we are friends

The relationships you have with your clients will often be tested and the main reason this happens is because there is a horse involved - the client's horse! You need to always remember that the reason people are boarding at your stable to begin with is because they needed a place to keep their horse. Sometimes if a friend comes to board at your barn the relationship can become even more strained. They will see a different side of you as the businesswoman that they haven't experienced before. It will also put a new twist on things when they become a paying client. Were they a client first and then became a friend or a friend first that later became a client? Both scenarios can come crashing down with friendships lost if you are not careful as the professional.

Whether a horse is coming in with kick or bite marks or many other issues that will come up it will always come back to you as the professional. What you decide to do to rectify a situation will either be great for the client or leave them upset because they don't like the decision you made. At this point it doesn't matter how close you are as friends. The friendship will suffer and feelings may be hurt if the outcome is not what the client anticipated.

Men do not seem to go through all these relationship issues that women go through when it comes to running a business. They are definitely created differently and there have been countless times when my husband has said to me that I shouldn't have gotten so involved. Rationally I know that I shouldn't get involved in some situations but my heart has told me differently and often I have followed my heart only to regret it later. My husband was right many times.

This will be part of your journey as a professional horsewoman where you will makes mistakes in your judgement and learn from the heartache that follows. We all go through it and it will change you in many ways. Without boundaries your judgment can easily become clouded regarding the decisions you make for your horse business.

Lessons learned

Over time you will learn to be more discerning in what you share with your clients and you will learn to think twice before you open your mouth about certain things. You might find yourself feeling frustrated in the beginning because you will have this internal struggle going on inside of you. You will want to continue in your old habits and join in but this little voice will start to guide you and tell you when it is time to walk away. This is all part of maturing as a businesswoman. You might feel like you have no one to talk with about the issues you are having so this is when you need to find someone outside your business to share those kinds of conversations with. Not your clients! All professionals go through this no matter what they choose for a career. You are going to go through a time of learning with lessons along the way and all of it will help mold you into a much more rounded professional businesswoman.

You can still be friends with your clients and do things with them outside of the barn. But just remember that until the day they move their horse or take them out of your training program, your role as the barn manager or horse trainer will need to come first and the friendship will need to be second. It is a difficult thought to accept but it is reality when they are still writing you checks for your services each month.

The one thing I want to express more than anything is that throughout your career you are going to experience many different opinions and situations where your clients don't like the choices you make and how you choose to do things. This will also include gossip conversations or your choice **not** to be part of such conversations. It is going to happen and there is no way to avoid it. As a woman you are going to feel hurt but as a seasoned professional you will learn to deal with this better as time goes on and not take it so personally. You will get through it and one day you will be glad you decided to put some boundaries in place.

I believe that when boundaries are in place they are good for your business and good for the relationships that you have at your barn. You will be pleasantly surprised how much healthier your barn will be when you have established boundaries for yourself and your clients. Boundaries will keep you from crossing over to a place you should never go and help you avoid more problems down the road. Over time you will learn what boundaries work best for you and the longer you run your horse business the more confident you will become at maintaining healthy boundaries.

There is a bright side

I knew as I was writing this chapter that it might be a little discouraging for many women reading this that are involved in a horse business that consumes their life. I want you to know there is a bright side!

As you grow as a businesswoman and become more confident in how you run your barn you will continue to establish many wonderful relationships with your clients. You will laugh and cry with them and do things outside the barn with them often. You will enjoy their company and they will enjoy yours. The interesting thing is that once you have established boundaries for your barn and business they will understand what those boundaries are just by how you conduct yourself in all circumstances and conversations. They will quickly realize that there are certain things that shouldn't be talked about when you are around. They will respect you enough not to put you in an uncomfortable situation. You will also learn to do the same for your clients and when that happens a new kind of relationship will grow and it will be much healthier for all involved and better for your business.

I want to encourage you to have fun with your clients and get to know them. Do many things with them and enjoy each other. Just remember at the end of the day that it is still your business and it is your responsibility to keep those boundaries in place so that feelings don't get hurt and the relationship suffers.

This will be probably one of the most difficult parts of your career to get a firm grasp on. Even after years of running my barn I still have to remind myself when I am caught up in the moment to watch what I say. Don't be too hard on yourself if you blow it. I have blown it many times! Own up to it and move forward and always learn from each mistake. You will become wiser about what is appropriate to talk about as a professional the longer you do it. It does get much easier. You will never regret having reasonable boundaries established for you and your clients.

Your Personal Thoughts and Goals

1. *What type of atmosphere do you want to have in your barn? Make a list of problem areas that you would like to change as it relates to boundaries and gossip.*

2. *What would you like to change about yourself and how you handle gossip and boundaries? Do you feel you are learning and growing in these areas? This is a hard one ladies but I encourage you to be honest and look deep inside yourself about situations you found yourself in.*

Your Personal Thoughts and Goals

3. I encourage you to find a mentor or friend who has been a positive person in your life to share some of your struggles and set some new goals and a timeframe for your business. Goals are always a good thing to keep us motivated.

~15~

Hanging On to the Wrongs

"A woman who can forgive shows that she possesses strength, compassion and strong leadership well beyond what the world would define. She is truly an amazing woman."

I have struggled in the past with letting go of some of the wrongs that I felt were done to me. In my heart I had forgiven the person that had hurt me but sometimes those old feelings of hurt and resentment start to creep back in. It's like they are waiting for me to put my guard down and they attack when I am at my weakest. I believe most women are very good at hanging on to memories and old feelings both good and bad and letting go can be extremely difficult.

Over the years of running our boarding facility I have learned so much about myself and some of it wasn't pretty and it was hard at times to acknowledge. Much of it was about me and how I handled conflict of any kind. Becoming a business owner forced me to take a hard look at how I dealt with my emotions when my feelings were hurt by someone. I found myself doing a lot of soul searching.

When you are running your barn you are going to come across many different types of people with many different personalities. You will have disagreements with clients about the care you provide the horses and the decisions you make at your stable and that will be just the beginning. You will have clients that don't like the way you do certain things and they may even challenge you. Things will be said that you will find offensive and at times the hurt will cut you to the core. It is all part of working with people and the healthiest thing you can do for yourself and your business is to resolve the issue and let it go. **I am not saying at all to let a client walk all over you and treat you with no respect.** There are times when the disrespect has crossed the line and it is best to ask a client to leave and move their horse. But for the unusual occurrence with a normally easy going client you need to look at the entire picture of what happened to begin with. Once you have worked out the disagreement or misunderstanding you need to let it go and that means letting go of the hurtful words that were spoken to you. Is it easy? Absolutely not! But it is so important. If you are willing to learn from each argument or confrontation then managing your emotions will become easier with time and you will become a much better businesswoman inside and out.

Most people say things in the heat of the moment that they later regret and as the professional I want you to take the high road and move forward. I have been very blessed over the years to have boarders that have been extremely forgiving of me when I have lost my temper and they forgave me quickly. I have learned from their example when I was the one at fault. By letting go and forgiving others it will free you to run your horse business without the weight that anger and resentment carry.

> *By letting go and forgiving others it will free you to run your horse business without the weight that anger and resentment carry.*

The only one you are hurting is you

I believe the saying is true — "If you are not able to forgive then the only one you are hurting is you." When I have hung on to a transgression that has been done to me it festers inside of me and it can actually make me physically sick. It will wear you down emotionally and it will start to skew your judgement in the decisions you make for your horse business. If you get to this point then it would be fair to say that bitterness is starting to creep into your life and it will have a huge negative impact on your personal and professional life. Don't let it get that far!

I know there are going to be the rare exceptions where the situation is not going to resolve itself and the client will have to leave your barn. That is all part of running a business but you can still act professionally. I have run into previous boarders throughout the years that were very hurtful when they were at my barn and it is the greatest feeling in the world when forgiveness takes over and I have no ill feelings towards that person. In fact, it is totally liberating! It is good for you as a professional and great for you as a person. You will be amazed at how much you will change on the inside when you learn to let it go.

As you grow and you start to experience many different kinds of people with your business you will realize that most people are good people that don't intentionally mean to hurt you. I have learned throughout the years that usually the people that are hurtful and say mean things to others are hurting themselves deep inside and are very unhappy. That has helped me to move forward and even have compassion for that person. Remember that you don't always know what is going on in your client's personal life.

It is true that a client might need to leave your barn over something they have done and if it gets to that point remember you will most likely run into them in the future. Learning to forgive and let go will be the healthiest thing you can do for yourself. You will feel the weight lifted off your shoulders when you can accomplish this and you will experience an incredible peace that others will notice.

I have found that when I am struggling to forgive someone that has hurt me, I don't have the strength to do it on my own and that is when I need to take it to the Lord daily in prayer. He has helped me overcome bitterness and anger that I otherwise would have held on to.

Your Personal Thoughts and Goals

1. Are you hanging onto something negative that someone has done to you? If so, today I encourage you to dig deep inside and let it go for your own health and well-being. I know it is painful and I have been there but once you let it go you will start to change and grow in a wonderful new way. Take baby steps and pray!

Your Personal Thoughts and Goals

2. *List some of the ways you see yourself changing and growing as it relates to your personal growth and forgiveness. How has this impacted your horse business? Do you see a difference in your relationships with your clients? Be proud of even the smallest step or gesture. They are all equally important in your personal growth.*

~16~

Don't Forget About the Horse

"When we are young we dream of the horse like they are a magical beast created just for us. As we grow up our love deepens so much that we are willing to give up all comforts just to call one of these beautiful equines our very own. When we become much older we realize just how fragile these magnificent horses truly are and our thoughts consume us daily to make their life as comfortable as possible until it is time to say good-bye. Thank you God for the gift of the horse."

There is so much that has been written over the years about the horse and if you are anything like me then you could easily fill up your library with books on every riding discipline to every breed and never get tired of reading about them. And then of course there are all the beautiful stories that will make you cry in the sad parts but will open your mind to dreams you never thought possible.

Owning a large boarding barn has opened my eyes to so much regarding horses and how they interact with each other daily and even how fragile they are in so many ways. I had worked at a couple of barns throughout my life and horse behavior was not a surprise to me but when I became the barn owner the pressure to make sure the horses got along was much greater. The care that I felt they needed to be happy and healthy was easy for me to provide but that didn't guarantee that they would get along in the herds or be well-behaved in their stalls. As new horses came to our farm they also brought with them many different issues and I began to see the full scope of the horse and how they are truly individual in all ways. Each with their own quirks and personality and you often can visualize what type of child or adult they would be if they were human! It's a funny way to look at it but I have found myself doing that a few times over the years with a few and it always makes me smile or laugh out loud every time. I was about to learn about horses in a much more intimate way and I would grow and find out so much about myself in the process. Most of it was good but there were some very hard lessons along the way.

From fantasy to reality

My days of dreaming about horses and what they could do for me and my happiness changed after we opened our barn. I became consumed with the challenge to make sure each horse felt safe and content whether in outdoor board twenty-four hours a day or stall board at night and turnout in herds during the day. Each boarding situation we offered came with its own issues to work through depending on the horses that were boarded at our barn. It was constantly changing because we had a high turnover of horses during the first couple of years of business and that meant there were constant changes in the herds. I was learning more about horse management than I had learned in all my time working at other barns and stables put together. I was starting to look at the horse in a new and refreshing way. There were even times that I started to feel sorry for the horse and all the things that some of them will endure throughout their life. I had never noticed it before until I was seeing it daily. I couldn't get away from it even when I was up in my house because I could look out my window and see what many of the horses were doing both good and bad.

As you start to operate your horse business you will begin to experience a new way of appreciating each horse in your care. Most of them will belong to your clients (unless you start collecting them which is easy to do!) and with that will come an added pressure and responsibility because you have been entrusted with the care of another person's love of their life. You might feel uneasy at first but the longer you care for your clients' horses the more comfortable you will become with your role as caretaker at your barn.

You are going to grow in so many areas and your journey as an equine professional might hit some rough spots as you experience the heartache that will come when tragedy hits your barn. You will feel sadness so deep when a horse needs to be put down that was in your care and many questions will go through your head during and after euthanasia. You will wonder if you did everything that could be done to comfort the horse. You will ask yourself if you did everything possible to comfort the owner that lost the horse. You will find yourself in uncharted territory the first time you need to stand strong for the owner of a very sick or injured horse and you are waiting for the veterinarian to come while knowing what the end results will be. You will learn to comfort and be strong all at the same time and you will become the rock that your clients need in times of tragedy.

> **You will learn to comfort and be strong all at the same time and you will become the rock that your clients need in times of tragedy.**

You will not always agree

You will not always agree with the client's care and management practices of their horse. You may at times find yourself dealing with difficult emotions because of the things you see happening to a horse that you don't agree with. You will need to decide how you want to handle or address care issues to preserve the integrity of your barn practices. The great part about being the barn owner is that you can make the rules for what is allowed and not allowed when it comes to the treatment of horses at your stable. The hard part will be confronting the person about the treatment in question and you will grow tremendously as an equine professional with each occurrence. As your barn gains a certain kind of reputation (you know people will talk) you will deal less and less with the undesirable treatment of horses at your place because the word on the street will be that you won't tolerate it. That is a great thing to establish!

You will watch horses being bought and sold. Most of the new owners will be wonderful but then there will be the one person that drives off with the horse they just purchased and you know deep down inside that the horse is going to have a very hard life ahead and there was nothing you could do because you didn't own the horse.

As a woman these emotions are pretty tough to deal with. I have seen so much good at our barn but I have also witnessed some pretty heartless stuff and years later it still bothers me. As a professional you can somewhat control what kind of barn you want but then something new will happen and you will be caught off guard. I have definitely become more vocal and less tolerant over the years when I see something that I feel is harmful to a horse at my barn and if I lose a boarder over the issue it doesn't bother me anymore.

Neglect and mistreatment of horses is a side of the industry that is extremely difficult to deal with but you will change so much throughout the years and become very strong and even assertive when you see things that you do not approve of. You will grow as a professional and the things you used to tolerate or maybe just ignored because it was too difficult to address will become much easier to manage because you will feel a deep sense of responsibility that will overcome any fears you have. You will start to look at the bigger picture of your business, people and the horses in your care. What happens at your place will affect everyone and you will quickly realize that it's not just about you anymore.

Horses act just like kids!

Horses (especially geldings) are like a bunch of kids. They play hard and get themselves into trouble at times. They will all have at least one issue or quirk and some will annoy you while others will make you laugh. You would like to think you love them all equally but the truth is you will secretly have your favorites! You will learn to appreciate them all in a special way and even though some will be easier to handle than others you will never skip a beat as you navigate through each horse. Getting to know the horses will become second nature as the years go by and what may have seemed overwhelming at first will become such a natural part of your chore time or training program.

> *You would like to think you love them all equally but the truth is you will secretly have your favorites!*

You are going to change and start to appreciate the differences about each horse in your care and it will have very little to do with papers, breeding or athletic abilities. At one time in your life you may have valued the horses that could jump high or perform high level dressage in a category by themselves as they deserve to be admired for their strength and athletic ability. Over time you will come to admire and truly appreciate the horses that make your job easier on a daily basis and you will admire them for many simple reasons and often newfound attributes.

> *Over time you will come to admire and truly appreciate the horses that make your job easier on a daily basis and you will admire them for many simple reasons and often newfound attributes.*

The horse that is quiet as you lead him out and waits patiently while you take off the halter has a wonderful attribute that you will appreciate so much over time. You will be thankful for the horse that doesn't kick or chew the wood in the stall and even the ones that keep their stall nice and tidy will make your day easier especially when you are cleaning it. You will appreciate a horse that doesn't try to bite you as you walk him to his paddock. You will adore the horse that gets along with everyone in his herd and seems to know how to stay out of trouble! You will fall in love with the horses that are calm and patient and look at you with eyes that tell you that they are ready to come in but will wait quietly until it is their turn. Don't get me wrong, I love all the horses at my barn but there are some that are more challenging than others when handling daily. It is all those little things that will make your job easier or harder and you will find yourself appreciating the simple everyday things that you do with horses.

You will know the horses at your barn better than the owners know them when it comes to eating, drinking and even stall cleaning! You will know how they act in their herd and if they are dominant or at the bottom of the herd. You will be able to tell the confident horses from the ones that try to act confident but really are very insecure. You may not know much about what each horse is like to ride but you will know their eating habits just like you know your own children and you will be able to tell in a split second if one of the horses looks off and seems like he is not feeling well. You will grow a sixth sense and you will become extremely attuned to the horses at your barn and you will love every minute of it.

Working with horses individually and in herds is such an integral part of the job and the feeling you get from it all will be something that you can't explain even when you try. Care and herd management will come so naturally just like a mother's instincts for her children. Your confidence is going to sky rocket about horse care and herd management and you will feel so proud inside when it all comes together.

The best part of it all

Being a professional horsewoman means doing many jobs in your line of work that you are not crazy about but you know they need to get done. It will mean paperwork, emails and giving tours. It will mean solving issues with clients and working through problems at the barn. There is a side of any business that is not fun but it is vital to keeping the business going.

Here's the best part of all. After the paperwork is done and emails have been answered you will head out to the barn and that is when you will remember why you got into this crazy business to begin with. You will hear a nicker and your heart will leap for joy as you walk down the barn aisle and you will then realize that you have the best job in the world and you will fall in love all over again with each and every horse at your barn.

The journey you will take as a professional horsewoman will change so much and that will include everything you do with horses throughout your life. You might change how you manage horses over the years and you are likely to learn many new things about giving the best care possible for each horse and their special needs. You will find out that the learning never stops and I encourage you to embrace the educational opportunities that are available. The horses will learn to trust you and look for you as you walk down the barn aisle and you will learn to trust yourself and your competence. You will gain a wonderful confidence and feel good about the decisions you make for the horses in your care and that is an incredible feeling. I believe after all these years I have fallen in love with horses even more!

Your Personal Thoughts and Goals

1. Write down some goals for things you would like to improve on with the care and chores at your stable.

2. List some areas of horse care where you feel you need to learn more about food, nutrition, herd management etc.

Your Personal Thoughts and Goals

3. *Make a list of a few horses and the special attributes they have that don't involve papers, breeding or confirmation. Make this about their personality and behavior and how it makes your job easier daily. After you have made the list I encourage you to let their owners know of some of these wonderful qualities their horse has. It will make their day!*

~17~

I Have Changed With Age

"When the years have given you wisdom it often will open your eyes to a different way of seeing things. That is when you will become rejuvenated and find new mountains to climb!"

I have often asked myself over the years why some barns and professional horsewomen are so successful and many others are struggling? I don't believe there is one clear reason but I do believe the most successful professionals have a few things in common.

I have the best job in the world or should I say two jobs. I have a boarding barn that I love working at every day and now I have the opportunity to go to other barns and help the owners improve their barn and business and make it more efficient and successful. There is something wonderful about walking into a horse barn. No two barns are alike and they are all beautiful in their own way.

I have learned that the horse businesses that improve the fastest with the issues they have do so because the barn owner has decided to make the needed changes and stick by them even if the changes are very difficult at the time. Often it is the barn owner/manager that needs to do some serious changing inside and that can be very hard for anyone to hear. It is hard to look at yourself and admit that many of the problems you are having in your business could be caused by you. I have been there and found it very humbling and even painful while I was going through it.

> *The horse businesses that improve the fastest with the issues they have do so because the barn owner has decided to make the needed changes and stick by them even if the changes are very difficult at the time.*

Every woman will go through this as she is running her business. If she wants to improve how she runs her horse business then there will come a time when she needs to look at herself objectively and see how she can improve everything. If you are willing to learn along the way then you will look back one day and everything will become clear and you will appreciate the journey. It is not an easy road to take but if you stay on track and learn and grow from each situation, that is when you will see the most growth inside of you. That is when the changes happen.

The early years

There are parts of the first three years of running our boarding facility that I truly can't remember. I was on auto-pilot much of the time and between working at the barn and having a second job there wasn't much left for anything else.

I was living the dream on the outside but my life was a mess professionally. I was insecure and lacking confidence in my decisions regarding the barn and our business. We had extremely high turnover and drama was killing our barn. I wasn't telling my boarders how things were going to run- instead they were telling me how the barn was going to run by their actions. My rules were ignored and getting paid for board was a waiting game every month. The list could go on and on but I am sure you get the picture. When they say that the first few years of any new business are the hardest they are not kidding!

When I finally hit bottom and realized I had to make major changes for my personal life and business, I knew they had to start with me first. No more blaming my boarders and playing the victim. The only reason I was having so many issues in the barn was because I was allowing it. I was mentally exhausted all the time because I had not taken control of all the problems that existed in our barn and it created more work than it should have.

Let me be very clear in saying that working extremely hard is part of owning and running your own business especially in the early years of operation. **Don't be afraid of hard work but understand that as time goes by the work should start to become easier and you should be able to find time here and there to relax and rejuvenate.** Often the job doesn't become easier even after a few years and that is when a person gets burned out and wants to quit. I believe this happens to so many businesswomen because they haven't worked through all the issues they are having. It is very hard and I understand this.

I am so glad those years are behind me. I had to grow a lot and make many mistakes along the way but those mistakes are what changed me along with my willingness to learn each and every day. It is a journey and you will go from an insecure woman who is trying to run a business to a confident businesswoman who takes control of her barn and runs it with integrity, honesty and leadership. Is it an easy journey? Of course not but the end results will be so much sweeter because you had to work harder to get there.

> *It is a journey and you will go from an insecure woman who is trying to run a business to a confident businesswoman who takes control of her barn and runs it with integrity, honesty and leadership.*

It is very true that anything worth having is worth fighting for and that will be so true for your horse business. There will be times when you want to yell and cry and you will learn to do it in the privacy of your home away from your clients. You are going to learn to make extremely difficult decisions that will not be pleasing to some of your clients and you will stick by your decisions and eventually feel good about them. You will grow with each decision whether it was a good one or bad one and you will keep moving forward.

One day you will look back after many years have gone by and realize that it was all part of the process and those bad times are what turned you into the confident woman that you are. You will look back at those turbulent times and actually be glad they happened because those were the times that enabled you to grow the most on the inside. You will never jump for joy that they happened but you will know that they were necessary to help you become all that you could be.

What will separate you from the rest

When you choose to make the changes needed inside to grow as a businesswoman that is what will separate you from the rest. Why do some barns grow and become extremely successful while others struggle to stay alive? Why do some horse trainers have so many clients that they need a waiting list while others are working two other jobs just to pay the bills? The answers will be different for each person but I do believe that if you asked, many of them would tell you that part of their success came from the willingness to change and learn from every mistake. That is what set them apart. They were not afraid to change the areas in their own life that needed changing when it came to how they ran their business. They were determined to succeed and they never gave up or quit.

Don't ever stop learning

My father used to tell me when I was a young girl to learn something new each and every day. It was his way of telling me to never stop growing and learning in all areas of my life. This is so true and I still think about his words every time I learn something new about myself and my business.

I have changed over the years and part of it is because I am getting older (which I hate to admit) but much of it was because I desperately wanted our business to be successful and have clients who loved being at our farm. Yes I am less tolerant in some areas when it comes to following the rules and safety issues but in many ways I am more understanding of mistakes and misunderstandings because I know my boarders are learning and growing and they are also on their own special journey with their horse. When you have clients that respect the rules you have established and you are able to let go and let them learn independently with their horse, you will find a barn that is full, healthy and has a relaxed atmosphere. That is a very special barn.

We are all on a path whether it is as a horse trainer or the owner of a boarding stable or a variety of other wonderful careers in the horse industry. The best part of all is that we are all in this together and supporting each other through the difficult times in our careers is so important. We might be taking separate paths in the horse industry but we are all connected in some way or another because of the horse and there is a very good chance our paths will cross at one time or another.

One more special thought – People change careers often especially during their younger years. I am no exception. Don't be scared to look at all your options and what is out there. There are so many wonderful careers in the horse industry and you might experience a few of them as you change and grow yourself. It happened to me in my fifties!!

Your Personal Thoughts and Goals

1. List some areas that you would like to change about yourself.

2. What changes have you noticed in yourself since you started your horse business?

Personal Thoughts and Goals

3. What goals do you have for yourself and where you want to be five years down the road? Do you see yourself in the same career choice? Are there other careers in the horse industry that you are thinking about?

~18~

They Grow Up So Fast

"Today let's celebrate the women who have raised horses, barns and businesses while raising their families."

One of the hardest things for any businesswoman to do is juggle her family life with her business. It is extremely challenging at times especially if you are raising children in the midst of all of it. No one could have prepared me for this challenge and I would venture to say that most working mothers feel the same way.

Having a horse farm seems like the perfect life and in many ways it is but it is still a business. That means that someone needs to run it and make sure everything is taken care of in a timely manner. The books and paperwork that come with any business still need to be done and that is after the chores are done and the horses are cared for. There are possible new clients to meet and tours to give and there are vet calls for sick or injured horses. The phone will ring often and the text messages will be waiting no matter the time of day. I never knew there was so much that needed to be done daily to keep our business up to date in all areas. To this day the horses are still the easiest part.

When we built Vinland Stables my girls were still in elementary school. My youngest daughter was only five years old. Both girls needed me and even though I was working at home to them I wasn't working at all. They didn't understand that my job was a real job and that was how mommy and daddy got paid. To them I was playing and it didn't matter who I was talking with I would soon see two little girls coming into the barn to find out when I was going to make dinner because they were hungry. Because our boarding facility was new and I was learning how to run a business (the hard way might I add) I was out in the barn much more than I ever envisioned. I soon started to feel a great pressure tugging at me from both my children and the business. I slowly had to figure out how to balance the barn, business and my family and it was not easy on most days in the beginning. I now believe that many working mothers feel this same pressure no matter what line of work they are in.

Great kids

My oldest daughter just graduated high school this last year and as I reflect on the last ten years I realize that both my daughters handled being part of a family business pretty well. They have learned what sacrifice is and they didn't complain (most of the time) when we needed to leave parties early so we could get home to do evening chores. We left holiday gatherings early and many other family functions and that was our life. I worked hard to try to balance it out by playing games with them and watching movies together. We may not have gone out often but we were home together as a family.

I believe having our horse business has taught my daughters a lot about commitment, responsibility and the value of hard work. They certainly have a very realistic view of what running a horse boarding business is all about. They both have expressed that they do not want to carry on in the business and I am completely fine with that. I want them to spread their wings and do whatever life is calling them to do. Looking back I don't think I would change a thing about how we raised them. Of course I wanted to be able to buy them more, as any parent feels, but it really isn't the most important thing in life.

It is not always about the money and even though to most kids the grass always looks greener on the other side (mine included), I believe having our horse business has taught my girls so many valuable lessons about life and relationships and you can't purchase that in the mall.

Don't put too much pressure on yourself

The best thing I did as I got a handle on running my barn was to make it a priority to spend more time with my girls. I learned to prioritize things that could wait in the barn and when I started doing that my life change for the better. My family became a priority again and the barn and business did just fine. I stopped micro-managing my boarders and how they were doing things when they came out to see their horse. The barn ran just as smoothly without me when I was doing family stuff. It took me a few years to figure this all out but once I did it truly improved my life and my family's life.

Today I encourage you as a woman, wife and mother to make the time to spend with your family because you can never get those years back. Your barn, horses and clients will be just fine. One day your children will be graduating from high school and you don't want to look back and have regrets.

As women, wives and mothers we are really good at loading on the guilt in our lives and putting so much pressure on ourselves to be everything to everyone. We think we are indispensable in all areas. It can cause us a great deal of stress and even make us physically sick if we are not careful. There are going to be times when you need to be in the barn and there will be many times when you don't and the barn, horses and your clients will be fine! Find a balance that works for you and your family and watch how the pressure diminishes.

> *There are going to be times when you need to be in the barn and there will be many times when you don't and the barn, horses and your clients will be fine!*

I believe as women we can do it all if we have a healthy balance of self, family and business. Your children will grow up so fast and if you are not careful you will have missed some of the most incredible and fun years in your family's life You might make many mistakes when it comes to running your horse business but you don't want to make a huge mistake when it comes to time with your family. Your clients and horses can manage for a while without you.

Your Personal Thoughts and Goals

1. List some of the struggles you are having in finding time between family and business. Do you find yourself in the barn with clients more often then you should be?

2. Today I encourage you take baby steps towards a healthy balance of work and family time. Write down some goals in this area to get control of your time.

Your Personal Thoughts and Goals

3. *It is very easy to be physically in your home and with family and have your mind on business and the barn. Don't go there! Work on separating the two unless it is an emergency. Often times this is because we are micro-managing our clients and we want to know everything they are doing. Make a list of the most important things in your life that you value and start to get a healthy perspective of what business ownership is all about. Your family will thank you for it!*

~19~

What is Important in Your Business?

"If you are willing to dig deep to find out what is truly important in your business, you will soon find out that it's not what you originally thought."

You are going to go through many stages while running your horse business and what was very important to you when you first started will change along the way. Part of this will be because you have grown in confidence and part of it will be because, over time, you will have a much clearer direction on where you want your business to go. Even after you change many things in your horse business, time will go by and you will start to look at it differently again because you have grown and changed. I believe most women will experience this throughout their career. Finding out what is truly important in your personal and professional life means you are growing and evolving and that is healthy for any business and it is good for us as women.

More arenas, more amenities!

When we first opened our barn I was excited and nervous all at the same time. Here we had this big beautiful barn and I worried that we were not going to fill all the stalls and that of course would mean we would struggle to pay our bills. I was constantly comparing my barn to all the other boarding places in our area because I didn't feel like we were good enough. I would look at what other barns had to offer and I pressured my husband many times that we needed the same things as our competitors to keep up with them.

We spent money we didn't have to build a third very large riding arena and buy a round pen when they both could have waited for a couple of years. We were offering services for free just to give us an edge and it started to burn us out. Our barn hours were extremely long and we cleaned stalls seven days a week. **I thought these things were what would attract people to our barn and they did BUT that was not why they stayed.** I believed at the time that these extras were very important for our business to be a success. I didn't see the big picture for quite a few years.

Figuring out what is important in your business is something that you should take a good look at but be prepared because it will change as the years go by. It will change because of your family and personal life. It will change because of the new ideas you have for the barn. It will change because you will start to relax about the things that you thought were important when you first started. When I look back ten years I realize how much I have changed and what I thought was important way back then, I now hardly acknowledge.

> *When I look back ten years I realize how much I have changed and what I thought was important way back then, I now hardly acknowledge.*

What is important in a business will be different for every woman running her own barn or equine program. The first thing you cannot do is compare your horse business to another. The second thing is to appreciate that as you age and your family grows that your personal needs are going to change and this will affect many aspects of your business. Imagine how much your life and priorities change as you go from having babies to watching your children go off to college. What an incredible journey!

Younger verses older

There is a lot to be said about starting a business when you are younger. When we are younger we have endless energy and we are bold. We tend to throw caution to the wind and we have a youthful optimism which is fantastic. There are many people who start businesses when they are young and they bounce back easier if it fails. As you become older you might still have a lot of energy but you start to slow down just a bit. You might be bold but you will think things out more thoroughly before you jump in. As we get older we might still take many chances but we will think about the risk involved much more because it will affect our family and lifestyle we have worked so hard to achieve.

Starting a horse business is great at any age and I have talked to women who in their forties and fifties are thinking about boarding horses. Some of them have even built barns and are jumping in with both feet ready to begin a new life and career. No matter your age your business will change in many ways and years down the road you might love the new changes and things you are doing with horses even better than what you began with.

Relaxing about things as you age

I have definitely mellowed about many things in my horse barn. We still maintain a very clean, highly organized barn and everything has a place. We still handle the horses and chores the same way we did ten years ago and it still works very well. There have also been many changes throughout the years and many of them might not be noticeable on the outside or to my boarders. Many of them have been emotional and mental changes for me and how I run our barn and business.

> *I have learned that having all the amenities in the world doesn't make a great barn. It's the people that make a great barn. What makes a great horse business are barn owners and managers that run their business with honesty and integrity and always put the horses' care first.*

I have learned that my boarders are trying their best to do things right and I need to lighten up at times. I have learned that they are going to make mistakes but if I am patient and explain things in a gentle way they will try harder not to make the same mistake twice. I have learned that having all the amenities in the world doesn't make a great barn. It's the people that make a great barn. What makes a great horse business are barn owners and managers that run their business with honesty and integrity and always put the horses' care first. I have learned that there is no perfect barn and you need to be okay with what you offer and stop comparing yourself to other places. There will always be a barn that is bigger and better and offers things that you might not ever be able to offer. And that is okay.

I have come to realize that my barn will not be the right barn for everyone and I am good with that now. What is more important is that the right people will find my place and be glad they board here. I have learned that keeping things simple is better for horses and if you keep that in mind then the horses in your care will settle in faster. I have learned some painful lessons about running a horse business and life goes on even when someone leaves and you must keep going. The best part is that you will be just fine.

> *I have learned some painful lessons about running a horse business and life goes on even when someone leaves and you must keep going. The best part is that you will be just fine.*

Today I want to encourage you to find what is truly important in your life and business. They go hand in hand more than you would ever believe. The longer you run your business the more you will grow as a businesswoman. What was once important to you might change and with that will come a renewed excitement for what is ahead. Don't ever forget that change can be a wonderful thing especially when you see how it can impact other people's lives for the better.

Your Personal Thoughts and Goals

1. List some areas of your horse business that you feel passionately about. Do you see your horse business changing in the future? (For example-you want to start a retirement boarding stable for senior horses)

Your Personal Thoughts and Goals

2. Sometimes changes can involve simplifying your life. How would you like to simplify your life? Be specific and honest because seeing it on paper helps us move forward with the actions.

~20~

Time to Reconnect With Friends

"A friendship is something that needs to be cared for. If left alone too long it will soon wither up and die."

This chapter was very important for me to write because I experienced firsthand what it was like to lose connection with very close girlfriends because of my business. What many women don't understand is how much their horse business will consume them if they allow it. Sometimes they don't realize this until years later and then they find out that their closest friends have moved on. It will be a very painful time in your life if you let it get to this point. I know this from experience and I will never go back to that place again.

Starting a horse business of any kind is different compared to other businesses for the one main reason that you are taking care of animals that need care seven days a week. The business never closes for

Sundays or holidays. As women we know this going into it and because we have a passion and love for horses we are willing to except that as a part of the deal. It is after all, more than just a career; it is a lifestyle that we gladly embrace because we are crazy about horses and absolutely love being around them.

It is after all, more than just a career; it is a lifestyle that we gladly embrace because we are crazy about horses and absolutely love being around them.

What I thought was enough in the beginning

In the beginning I was so busy with our barn and raising my girls that I couldn't squeeze another thing into my life. I had crammed it as full of barn stuff as I could and I paid a big price that I didn't see until years later.

Life continued to go on for my friends and their families and soon the time we spent with them at parties or outings stopped. For as long as I could remember David and I had always been involved in a weekly bible study with other couples. That was one of the first things to go after we started our business and we experienced the stress of the first couple of years. Between the long hours we were putting in and working seven days a week, we were just too tired to commit to another obligation. There just wasn't any time or energy left. At least that is how I was feeling.

> *There were people at my barn all day long so in the beginning I never felt lonely.*

There were people at my barn all day long so in the beginning I never felt lonely. I had a great time with my boarders and I became close with some of them but it was still a business relationship especially when the board check was due each month or issues needed to be addressed. The business always had to come first. It was awkward at times when dealing with issues that affected a client and soon I learned that many of the friendships were not solid enough to withstand the complex barn owner/client relationship. I soon started feeling lonely and isolated in many ways and I started to miss my close friendships outside the barn. I had to find a way to rekindle those relationships as it wasn't enough anymore just being at the barn all the time. Don't get me wrong, I have wonderful boarders at our barn and feel blessed every day for the relationships we have but it is still a business and I needed to separate myself from it once in a while.

> *The euphoria that you feel when you start your horse business will be astonishing but it will not fill the emptiness that you will have if you give up all you knew before you started your business.*

The euphoria that you feel when you start your horse business will be astonishing but it will not fill the emptiness that you will have if you give up all you knew before you started your business. Your friendships and the other activities (that are non-horsey) are a big part of who you are and when you abandon them all to start your business you will one day long for them. If you are feeling lonely and you have walked away from everyone that was part of your life before you started your business, I encourage you to rekindle those relationships. That is where you will find yourself again and the loneliness you were feeling will be long gone. Cherish those friendships you had before you started your horse business. Those relationships will be the rock you need to get you through the tough days you will experience now and then.

Now I feel complete

The healthiest thing you can do for yourself is to invest quality time with your close friends. Reconnecting with a couple of girlfriends that I have known for many years has completed me. Now I feel whole. We need that connection with other women and making time to nurture your friendships is something that I would encourage you to do.

I have a girlfriend that I meet for lunch at least once a month and if I had the time I am sure we could talk for hours and never run out of things to talk about. The best part is that we rarely ever talk about horses. We talk about other stuff like our marriages and kids and life. We talk about everything else under the sun except horses and it's refreshing. Your life will become very shallow and isolated if you don't ever venture out or talk about anything besides horses. I am still crazy about horses but I know that there is a huge world out there with so much more to experience and share with others.

Remember that life goes on and horses will be a major part of it but NOT the only part. I believe that once you get a healthy balance in your life and find time to reconnect with good friends you will start to feel whole and experience a profound sense of peace and rejuvenation that will be amazing. Today I want to encourage you to take time each month and spend it with good friends. Even when you don't think you have the time, make it happen! You will never regret it

Your Personal Thoughts and Goals

1. Do you ever feel lonely in your barn even though there are people all around you? Do you long to talk about something different than horses? If you answered yes to either question, then it is time to make some personal changes.

Your Personal Thoughts and Goals

2. Have you lost contact with a close friend that you knew before you started your horse business? Today I encourage you to try and rekindle some connections with friends who are outside the business. You won't regret it.

~21~

Someone to Confide In

"As professional horsewomen we should always be willing to listen to those who need to talk and be ready to encourage and offer advice when asked. If we can share our experiences both good and bad then we will have given hope to the next generation of professional horsewomen."

When we opened our boarding barn I really didn't know what I was doing when it came to managing a large barn and dealing with clients. My life became crazy overnight and many issues were popping up all over the place. The worst part was I didn't have anyone to talk to about the issues that were constantly bombarding me.

I couldn't talk with my boarders because they would not understand and they were paying clients. I didn't want them to panic thinking I didn't know what I was doing and it would cause far more problems if they knew our business was having so many issues. I couldn't talk with friends because they didn't understand the horse world and all that was involved with this life that we had chosen. I was afraid to talk with other barn owners in the area because I didn't know them and I didn't want to expose our problems. I couldn't find any books at the time that dealt with the issues I was dealing with when it came to our business and the effects the business was having on our finances and my marriage. I was trying to be a wife, mother and now a business owner and working with my husband at times made life even more stressful because we both had a lot to learn and we both handled the stress differently and often poorly.

The best thing David and I did during our second year of business was to meet with a therapist who also understood the complexity of couples that own and run a business together. It was what we needed to get a healthy perspective on what we were doing to each other as we were trying to keep the business operating successfully.

After talking with many women over the last few years I realize that most of them are just like I was when we first started out. They feel lost and they don't have anyone they can talk to about their business and how it affects their family and personal life.

Find a mentor

The smartest thing you can do for yourself and your business is to find a mentor. Find someone that has owned a horse business for many years and has a positive outlook on life and how they run their barn. Find someone who will be truthful with you in a loving and encouraging way. There are many people that will have a negative outlook so I would suggest skipping them!

> *The smartest thing you can do for yourself and your business is to find a mentor.*

Once you talk with someone who has traveled the road you are on you will find out that you are not alone at all! They will understand the frustrations you are experiencing and they will be able to give you positive constructive feedback because they will have likely gone through many of the issues you are going through. They will give you direction and help you develop a plan to move forward.

One of the challenging things about the horse industry is that there are no mentorship programs set up (that I could find) that help the new business owner through the early years of their horse business. Most other businesses have programs to help new managers work through the challenges they will most likely have to deal with and new teachers are usually paired with a more seasoned teacher for their first couple of years of teaching. Owning and running your own horse business can feel isolating at times especially if you rarely get off the farm except to run to the market or feed store. Let me be honest and tell you that you will have days where you feel like you are stuck on the farm and driving to the market will sound exciting! That is why you need to make this an area of importance for both you and your family. It is not good or healthy to feel isolated all the time especially if you are having problems in your business.

Today I encourage you to reach out to other equine professionals that have been successful in the business and see if they would be willing to talk with you. It might not be a common thing to do but you can be the one to get the ball rolling and in the process make some new friends. You might find out that they are happy to talk with you and they might enjoy sharing ideas. It is truly a win/win for everyone.

Even after many years of running our barn I still come across a new issue now and then where I need a second opinion. There are always going to be new things that will catch you off guard and even though they will become fewer as the years go by you might still shake your head occasionally at something that stumps your management skills. It is a part of life and business ownership. I am so glad I have other equine professionals that I can call and ask their opinion when something new comes my way. We all could use a mentor from time to time

Your Personal Thoughts and Goals

1. Do you have someone that you can talk to about the problems you are having in your business and personal life? If not, then I strongly encourage you to find a mentor who understand the business and who can help you work through the issues you are having.

2. Make a list of things you would like to talk to a mentor about? Write down both the good and bad because it will help them understand what you are going through and in turn they can help you.

Your Personal Thoughts and Goals

3.   *Write down your thoughts on how you have grown in this area especially after talking with a mentor or someone in the same equine business.*

~22~

Becoming a Confident Businesswoman

"Becoming a woman of confidence is truly a sight to behold. She is humble yet ready to lead and you will have contentment and peace knowing that the horse you love so dearly will be taken care of so completely."

Where does confidence come from? That is a great question and I believe as women we are always trying to figure out who and what impacts our confidence. Owning your own horse business will test you beyond your wildest imagination and put you in many situations where you have to make decisions despite lacking confidence to do so. You will not be given any other option and you will need to rise to the job ahead and not look back. The great thing about the whole process is even though you will start out with very little confidence, with every decision you make your confidence will grow. You probably won't even notice all the changes taking place in you until you reach about the fourth or fifth year of running your horse business.

Some women come across as extremely confident while others seem to lack even the basics for making decisions. We all know someone who can walk into a room and make a decision without hesitation; it just seems so natural for them. It's true that some of us show more confidence than others but we will experience the same struggles and issues at our barns. Nothing can replace hands on experience. Even though some people appear confident on the outside doesn't mean they have the experience to back up their confidence and they may be trembling on the inside. Don't let new experiences become something you avoid. Embrace them, for that is where you will gain your confidence.

> *Don't let new experiences become something you avoid. Embrace them, for that is where you will gain your confidence.*

Experience is worth its weight in gold

You can't put a price tag on experience and it doesn't happen overnight. I believe you need a couple of years of running your horse business to experience your career to the fullest. The best classroom you will have is right in your barn and your learning curve will amaze you during those early years.

Don't compare yourself to the other equine professionals out there. You can admire them and what they have accomplished but you need to remember that they started out as beginners just like you. They have lost their tempers and made poor decisions at times. They have laughed and cried and even thought about changing careers a time or two when they were having a really bad day. It happens to everyone and the ones that seem the most successful could probably give you some pretty good stories of their early years while trying to start their businesses. They might be the most confident professional horsewomen on the outside but when they are alone in their home with their family I am sure there have been evenings when they have contemplated many of the same thoughts that are going through your mind.

Confidence will come if you don't give up

Confidence is something that will come if you don't give up. As your confidence grows so will how you handle the many different situations you will encounter. You are going to learn to educate without criticizing and correct with gentleness. You will learn to encourage with honesty and comfort with strength. You will learn to forgive and let yourself be forgiven which is huge. You will learn to keep going when there is nothing left and the day was a disaster. When you do have a great day, enjoy it to the fullest! They might seem sparse at first but eventually the good days will outnumber the bad days and you will find your job becoming easier without realizing it at first.

You are going to learn to educate without criticizing and correct with gentleness. You will learn to encourage with honesty and comfort with strength. You will learn to forgive and let yourself be forgiven.

Then one day you will wake up and start to believe that you are good at what you do and you will feel like you are becoming a professional horsewoman. When that day happens you will never forget it! It is truly an unforgettable feeling that will leave you beaming on the inside.

Confidence comes from experience and you are going to get more than your share of it. Be patient and don't be too hard on yourself. We all start out as beginners in our journey to make our dreams come true. What an awesome journey it is!

Your Personal Thoughts and Goals

1. Do you find your confidence growing? Name some situations where your confidence was put to the test but you came out on top. List some areas where your confidence has grown and be specific. For example — herd management, client communication etc.

Your Personal Thoughts and Goals

2. What are you the most proud of today in how you run your horse business? What are some of the things you are still working on?

~23~

Learning To Relax and Laugh at Yourself

"They say that laughter is the best medicine but I believe that was meant for people who don't own a horse."

You did it! You started your horse business and you are living the dream. You are on a journey that is going to mold you and change you in ways that you will never expect and it is all incredible.

You will experience life as an equine professional and your womanly instincts will be part of it. You will make many decisions based on your emotions at first but you will grow and learn to make them as a businesswoman with less emotion and more good common sense. You will be completely exhausted at times and then have boundless energy and it all could be on the same day. You will have your feelings hurt more than a few times and you will learn to let it go and forget about it. You will make someone's day the best day ever when you call them and tell them you have an opening at your barn and they have been waiting a very long time to get in. You will feel proud when you hear their excitement and it will re-energize you.

> **You will make many decisions based on your emotions at first but you will grow and learn to make them as a businesswoman with less emotion and more good common sense.**

Your journey will take you through highs and lows and you will look back one day and be glad that you experienced all of it because each experience helped to mold you into the strong woman that you are. You will feel pretty one day and then you will wonder how you ever got so dirty the next! Your feminine side will be tested many times when you see your clients dressed up and looking gorgeous and you haven't put makeup on in days because there just wasn't time and who puts make-up on to do chores at 5AM anyways!

Working with horses is the greatest career in the world. You just need to keep things in perspective. Remember that you are living the dream that many of your clients would love to live. With that will come sacrifice along the way but also a peace and contentment knowing you are doing what you were meant to do and nothing can take that away from you.

Above all else

Above all else I want you to learn to relax when making decisions because they usually work out. Relax because you can't change the outcome of every situation and you can't control what others decide to do in life and that includes your clients. Relax because life is too short and you will miss many great opportunities and experiences if you are too busy to notice the beautiful things happening right around you. Relax and breathe because you are in it for the marathon not the sprint.

I also want you to learn that it is okay to laugh at yourself now and then. You are going to make decisions that later on you will wonder what you were thinking at the time. You might even think you momentarily lost your mind! When those times happen take a breath and laugh. Don't be so hard on yourself. We have all been there and had those moments where our brain disappears and we do something foolish. Pick up the pieces and move forward.

I still laugh at some of the crazy ideas I have had over the years. Some of them have truly bombed and some have worked out. That is what has made my journey as a professional horsewoman so much fun. Have a good laugh and enjoy each moment.

Remember that you are a woman with so much to offer. You give a depth to business ownership that will make your business incredibly special. Don't underestimate all that you bring to your barn and the horses and clients in your care. You were created to do amazing things in life and how wonderful it is that horses are a part of it. What an incredible journey you are on and as things change along the way you will grow and change along with them. Today I want to celebrate the professional horsewoman that you have become.

I want to wish you many blessings in all that you do for the horses and people in your life. You have made their life so much richer by taking a chance and following your dreams.

Your Personal Thoughts and Goals

Follow your dreams and start journaling all the incredible experiences because they will become wonderful memories. You are going to have a lot in this career with horses!!

Your Personal Thoughts and Goals

Sheri's Books and Website

You can catch Sheri's blog articles every week at

www.probarnmanagement.com

Sheri has written several books on horse barn management and inspirational books about horses and running a business. You can find all her books on her website at www.probarnmanagement.com and Amazon.com.

A Step By Step Guide To Starting And Running A Successful Horse Boarding Business (The comprehensive book of horse boarding and effective barn management)

The Total Horse Barn Management Makeover (Practical business wisdom for running your horse business).

Caring for Horses with a Servant's Heart (A daily devotional for the horse professional and the horse lover in all of us).

About the Author

Sheri lives in Neenah, Wisconsin. She has two daughters and she owns and operates Vinland Stables alongside her husband David. Sheri has been both a boarder and now a barn owner and has truly experienced life on both sides of the fence. For the last fourteen years Sheri has had the pleasure of taking care of other people's horses at her barn. After years of running a boarding facility she now does consulting for barn owners and managers that are working to improve their boarding operation. She is also a blogger and a speaker who enjoys talking with other professionals in all areas of the horse industry. In her free time she loves hanging out with her family and watching movies in the evening or getting together with friends. Life is pretty simple these days and she wouldn't have it any other way.

Printed in Great Britain
by Amazon

50447235R00115